LUZON

MINDORO

SAMAR

PANAY

LEYTE

NEGROS

BOHOL

MINDANAO

MOUNT APO

SULU
ARCHIPELAGO

MAKASSAR STRAITS

SULAWESI

MOLUCCAS

NEW GUINEA

BANDA SEA

SUMBAWA

FLORES

TIMOR

SUMBA

ARAFURA SEA

TIMOR SEA

PACIFIC OCEAN

N

SOUTH-EAST ASIA

INDONESIA

BRUNEI

SINGAPORE

THE PHILIPPINES

THAILAND

MALAYSIA

INDONESIA

BRUNEI

SINGAPORE

THE PHILIPPINES

THAILAND

MALAYSIA

SOUTH-EAST ASIA

By the Editors of Time-Life Books
With photographs by Michael Freeman

TIME-LIFE BOOKS · AMSTERDAM

TIME-LIFE BOOKS INC.

EDITOR: George Constable
Director of Design: Louis Klein
Director of Editorial Resources: Phyllis K. Wise
Acting Text Director: Ellen Phillips
Editorial Board: Russell B. Adams Jr., Dale M. Brown,
Roberta Conlan, Thomas H. Flaherty, Lee Hassig,
Donia Ann Steele, Rosalind Stubenberg, Kit van
Tulleken, Henry Woodhead
Director of Photography and Research:
John Conrad Weiser

PRESIDENT: Christopher T. Linen
Chief Operating Officer: John M. Fahey Jr.
Senior Vice Presidents: James L. Mercer,
Leopoldo Toralballa
Vice Presidents: Stephen L. Bair, Ralph J. Cuomo,
Terence J. Furlong, Neal Goff, Stephen L. Goldstein,
Juanita T. James, Hallett Johnson III, Robert H. Smith,
Paul R. Stewart
Director of Production Services: Robert J. Passantino

Editorial Operations
Copy Chief: Diane Ullius
Editorial Operations Manager: Caroline A. Boubin
Production: Celia Beattie
Quality Control: James J. Cox (director)
Library: Louise D. Forstall

LIBRARY OF NATIONS

This book was created in London for
Time-Life Books B.V.

EUROPEAN EDITOR: Kit van Tulleken
Assistant European Editor: Gillian Moore
Design Director: Ed Skyner
Photography Director: Pamela Marke
Chief of Research: Vanessa Kramer
Chief Sub-Editor: Ilse Gray
Editorial Production Co-ordinator: Nikki Allen
Assistant: Maureen Kelly
Editorial Department: Theresa John, Debra Lelliott

Series Editor: Tony Allan

Editorial Staff for *South-East Asia*
Editor: Gillian Moore
Researcher: Susan Dawson
Designer: Lynne Brown
Design Assistant: Julie Busby
Sub-Editor: Frances Dixon
Picture Department: Christine Hinze, Peggy Tout
Editorial Assistant: Molly Oates

Contributors: The chapter texts were written by:
James Clad, John Cottrell, Frederic V. Grunfeld, Alan
Lothian and Andrew Turton.

Correspondents: Elisabeth Kraemer-Singh (Bonn);
Maria Vincenza Aloisi (Paris); Ann Natanson (Rome).

CONSULTANT

Dr. Michael Williams is Senior Talks Writer with
the Far Eastern Service of the British Broadcasting Corporation. His Ph.D. thesis examined the
early history of Indonesian political movements
in west Java. He has travelled extensively in
South-East Asia and written several studies on
the region's politics and history.

PHOTOGRAPHER: Michael Freeman began
his photographic career after studying Geography at Oxford University. His pictures have
appeared in many magazines and books, including volumes in several Time-Life Books' series.
He is the author of a number of books on
photography.

ISBN 0-8094-5318-5
Library of Congress Catalogue Card Number: 86-61816

Impreso por:
Edime, Org. Gráfica, S. A.
(Móstoles) MADRID

Encuaderna: Larmor, S. A.
(Móstoles) MADRID

Depósito Legal: M. 2.937-1987
I.S.B.N.: 84-599-1888-2

IMPRESO EN ESPAÑA
PRINTED IN SPAIN

COVER: In Zamboanga, a port in the southern
Philippines, the still sea reflects a waterside
mosque. Most of the Philippines were converted
to Roman Catholicism by the Spaniards who
colonized them in the 16th century, but the
southernmost islands remained loyal to Islam.

FRONT AND BACK ENDPAPERS: A topo-
graphic map showing the major islands, mountain ranges and rivers of South-East Asia ap-
pears on the front endpaper; the back endpaper
shows the six countries of the Association of
South-East Asian Nations, with the principal islands and towns.

This volume is one in a series of books de-
scribing countries of the world — their natural
resources, peoples, histories, economies and governments.

CONTENTS

CONTRASTS IN SIZE AND WEALTH

1,919

With a total land area as large as that of India and a population greater than that of the U.S., the South-East Asian countries form a major geopolitical grouping. In territory and population terms, the giant is Indonesia—3,000 times as big as Singapore. But Indonesia is also the poorest, while Singapore's per capita national product puts it alongside Spain and Greece. Malaysia, with 16 million people, is the only country untroubled by overcrowding.

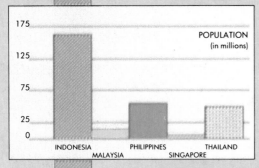

POPULATION
(in millions)

175
125
75
25
0

INDONESIA   PHILIPPINES   THAILAND
     MALAYSIA   SINGAPORE

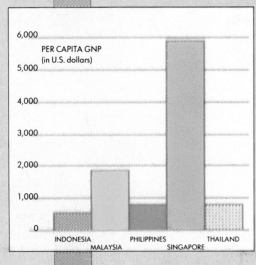

PER CAPITA GNP
(in U.S. dollars)

6,000
5,000
4,000
3,000
2,000
1,000
0

INDONESIA   PHILIPPINES   THAILAND
     MALAYSIA   SINGAPORE

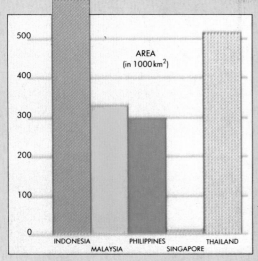

AREA
(in 1000 km²)

500
400
300
200
100
0

INDONESIA   PHILIPPINES   THAILAND
     MALAYSIA   SINGAPORE

Traffic and shoppers crowd Petaling Street in the Chinatown district of Kuala Lumpur, the

pital of Malaysia. The Chinese form substantial minorities in most South-East Asian cities, where many are influential members of the trading community.

ASSAULT ON THE WORLD'S OLDEST RAINFORESTS

PERCENTAGE OF LAND AREA FORESTED

100

80

60

40

20

0

PHILIPPINES
BRUNEI
INDONESIA
SINGAPORE
THAILAND
MALAYSIA

The rainforests of South-East Asia, the world's oldest, are surpassed in area only by those of Latin America. But they are being exploited at a rate that will consume them in a few decades if it continues unchecked. Pressure on resources is forcing farmers to clear virgin land for the plough, especially in Thailand, where the population has increased almost three-fold in the past 50 years. Logging companies cull valuable hardwoods, including teak, ebony and mahogany: South-East Asia supplies 70 per cent of the tropical wood consumed worldwide. Conservation in the area is in its infancy, and few replanting projects are under way.

Wayfarers in the Malay Peninsula cross a bridge slung between densely wooded hillsides, where towering evergreens form a canopy over lesser species.

heir 30 million years of existence, South-East Asia's rainforests have evolved a greater variety of flora than any other region in the world.

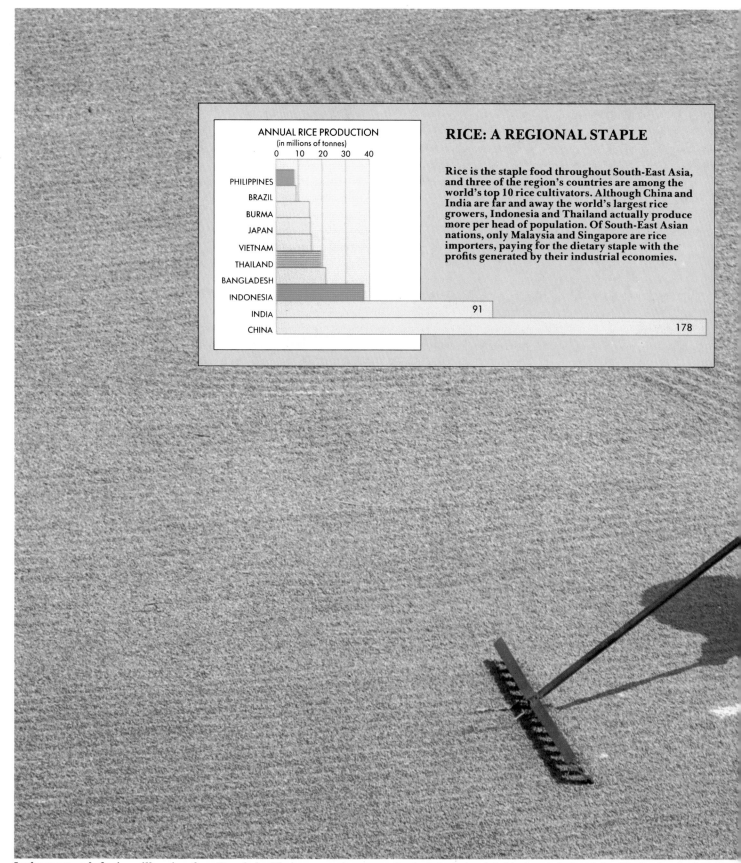

ANNUAL RICE PRODUCTION
(in millions of tonnes)

	0	10	20	30	40
PHILIPPINES					
BRAZIL					
BURMA					
JAPAN					
VIETNAM					
THAILAND					
BANGLADESH					
INDONESIA					
INDIA				91	
CHINA					178

RICE: A REGIONAL STAPLE

Rice is the staple food throughout South-East Asia, and three of the region's countries are among the world's top 10 rice cultivators. Although China and India are far and away the world's largest rice growers, Indonesia and Thailand actually produce more per head of population. Of South-East Asian nations, only Malaysia and Singapore are rice importers, paying for the dietary staple with the profits generated by their industrial economies.

In the courtyard of a rice mill upriver from Bangkok, a Thai woman rakes over unhusked rice being dried in the sun before it is milled and sacked. With on

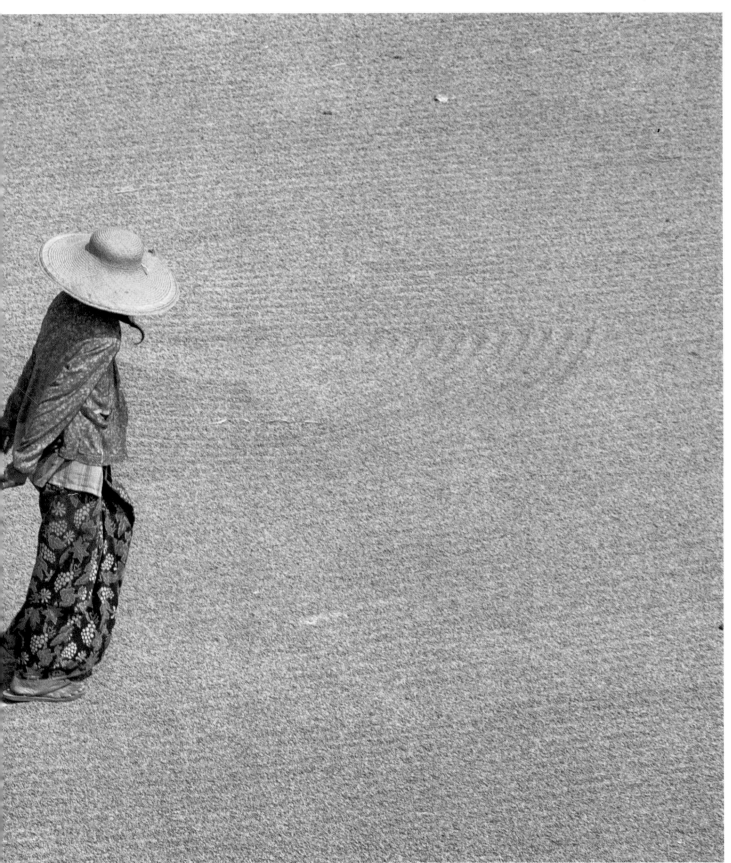

xth of the country under paddy fields, Thailand is the world's major rice exporter, selling almost one quarter of its production abroad.

Brightly coloured footwear covers the steps of a mosque in Brunei where Muslims have gathered for prayer. In both Brunei and Malaysia, Islam is the sta

...ligion, while in Indonesia it is practised by some 90 per cent of the population—many of whom, however, retain some indigenous beliefs.

THE BOUNTY OF THE OCEANS

Scattered over innumerable islands and peninsulas, the seagoing peoples of South-East Asia possess an invaluable resource in the 2,500 fish species that flourish in the surrounding tropical waters. Seafood is the region's major source of protein, and in most South-East Asian countries fish consumption is at least twice the world average.

Traditionally, local fishermen have gone out in sailing junks or outrigger canoes to take their catches with lines, traps or drift nets. Much of the yield is then eaten fresh, although in the hot, humid climate, methods were long ago also devised for preserving a surplus. The most characteristic is fermentation to yield a pungent sauce, but fish may otherwise be smoked or dried.

Since the 1960s, however, the region's small fishermen have had to compete with a rapidly growing fleet of trawlers. The result has been an increased yield everywhere in the region; in Thailand the catch rose tenfold in the dozen years to 1972, and a thriving export industry in frozen shrimps and squid and canned tuna developed. Since then, production has levelled off and there have been growing fears of overfishing.

Filipino fishing craft work the shallows near an island in the Sulu archipelago at the country's southern tip. The boats are motorized; the masts and the we

rope surrounding them serve only to hold in place the outriggers, which give the vessels stability.

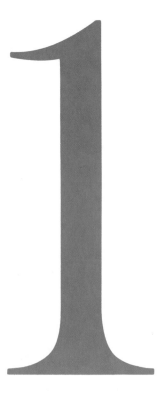

A RESOURCEFUL TROPICAL REGION

South of China, east of India: the description is at once vague and exotic. South-East Asia is certainly the latter, at least to Western eyes: lush, tropical, the home of scores of races and cultures. But the term is less vague than it once was, because "South-East Asia" has acquired a steadily more precise and confined meaning since the region first emerged as a political entity during World War II. At that time the phrase embraced a vast area: the great peninsula of Indochina, dangling like ripe fruit from the Asian landmass, and the enormous, equator-straddling archipelago to its south. Both of the regions were made up of many countries. In the peninsula, Burma, Thailand, the Malay States and French Indochina—comprising the lands now known as Vietnam, Laos and Cambodia—merged together in jungle-clad highlands. The thousands of islands in the archipelago included New Guinea, Borneo and the Philippines group.

Now, this broad geographical definition has largely been superseded by a more focused, geopolitical one. The term indicates specifically the six members of the Association of South-East Asian Nations (ASEAN): Indonesia, Malaysia, Thailand, Singapore, the Philippines and the sultanate of Brunei. The association was formed in 1967 as a protective response to the wars then plaguing Indochina.

For a quarter of a century before that date, the conflict in Vietnam had dominated the politics of the region. First, it was an anti-colonial struggle against the French, then a war between the new states of North and South Vietnam. In the late 1950s, the American government was drawn in; they first sent troops to the conflict in 1965. Both Vietnams suffered terrible destruction and at the end of the 1960s the fighting spilled across the region's notoriously fluid borders, submerging Laos and Cambodia in chaos, death and misery. The other South-East Asian nations looked on in horror, fearful that the contagion might strike them, too. Burma retreated behind the curtain of "Buddhist Socialism" and kept itself to itself, Thailand and the Philippines allied themselves strongly with the U.S., while Indonesia put its faith in the Non-Aligned Movement.

When ASEAN was founded, few regarded it as a chance for the beginning of a new regional polity. The five founder nations—Brunei was not yet a member—all shared anti-Communist sentiments and a more or less free-market approach to their economies; between them, however, lay a history of mutual bickering and even outright hostility. The Bangkok meeting that launched the association was strong on rhetoric and weak on substance, and no achievement of note marked the association's early years. The best it managed was a pious declaration in 1971 in favour of a "Zone of Peace, Freedom and Neutrality" in the area,

Amid the lush tropical vegetation of the Indonesian island of Bali, flooded terraces, newly planted with rice shoots, ascend a hillside. Rice is South-East Asia's staple food and the region's landscapes have been shaped over millennia by its cultivation.

17

1

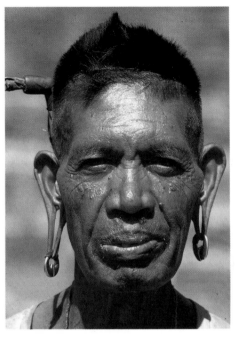  

without any hint of just how that aim would be achieved.

Sometimes, though, a crisis can help to forge a community, and ASEAN did grow into a practical and cohesive force, spurred on precisely because of the region's lack of peace, not to mention freedom and neutrality. The fall of the South Vietnamese capital Saigon in 1975 brought the end of the Vietnam War, but the ASEAN countries were left with a dangerous new neighbour whose million-man army and lavish military equipment gave ASEAN leaders sleepless nights. American withdrawal from Indochina was matched by an increasing Soviet presence. At the same time, China was still uncomfortably close and remained frighteningly unpredictable. Some of ASEAN's worst fears were realized in 1979 when Vietnam invaded Cambodia and when Hanoi's troops, preceded by hundreds

of thousands of refugees, arrived on Thailand's doorstep.

By then, however, ASEAN had at last closed ranks. Its foreign ministers began to hold annual meetings and soon discovered that jointly they could exercise far more diplomatic pressure than they ever could separately. The late 1970s, for instance, were the years of the so-called "boat people", the endless stream of refugees who fled Communist Vietnam—often with the connivance of Hanoi—and placed an intolerable strain on the neighbouring ASEAN economies. The ASEAN nations mounted an international campaign which had a twofold success: Vietnam grudgingly reduced the flood, and the major industrial nations recognized that refugee resettlement was a world and not a regional problem. In response to the invasion of Cambodia, ASEAN pursued a sustained diplo-

matic offensive that culminated in the United Nations refusing to recognize the Cambodian government supported by Vietnam and continuing to recognize the old government overthrown by the Vietnamese. By flexing its muscles, ASEAN had found its strength.

ASEAN is not a military alliance, although individual members usually work together willingly in that field. It is not even an economic alliance, on the lines of the European Economic Community; although there is much lip-service paid to the idea of co-operation, the member nations have yet to completely eliminate import duties on each other's goods, and less than 20 per cent of their trade is within ASEAN. A few joint projects have been set up—notably a giant fertilizer plant in Indonesia—but for the most part the member countries compete against one another to export primary

products to the rest of the world.

Essentially, ASEAN is a political alignment, a recognition of common interests by neighbouring countries. Until the need for a measure of political unity became apparent, there seemed to be little to draw them together. In their geography, race, religion and history, their economies and their politics, the countries of South-East Asia show some marked and keenly felt contrasts. Diversity, indeed, is one of the hallmarks of the region.

Indonesia is by the far the biggest of the ASEAN countries in both its area and population. It encompasses the world's largest archipelago—13,677 islands in all. Its most substantial territories are Sumatra, Kalimantan (the bulk of the island of Borneo) and Irian Jaya (the western half of the island of New Guinea). Much of Indonesia is

tropical rainforest and only thinly populated. But the volcanic, intensely fertile islands of Java and Bali support one of the world's highest population densities, and Indonesia's total population of more than 160 million is the fifth highest. The huge majority of Indonesians are of Malay stock—a race of small, brown-skinned people who arrived in the islands from the Asian hinterland 5,000 years ago. Most Indonesians are Muslims, though there are also millions of Hindus, Christians and other religious groups.

Long a Dutch colony, Indonesia declared independence in 1945. Since an attempted Communist coup in 1965, repressed savagely, the army has had a central role in the government.

Indonesia's northern neighbour, the Philippines, is another enormous archipelago. Its population of more than 50 million is scattered among 7,107

palm-fringed islands. Most Filipinos are of Malay stock, though not closely related to the Malays of Indonesia. A large Chinese minority has interbred extensively with the Malays.

The Philippines had the unique experience of being colonized twice: 300 years under Spain, which left most Filipinos Catholic, were followed by 50 years of American rule. Independence came in 1946. In 1965, Ferdinand Marcos was elected president and from 1969 until his hurried departure in 1986 he was a virtual dictator.

Next in size after the Philippines is Thailand, whose 50 million people inhabit more than half a million square kilometres on the Asian mainland. While mountains guard Thailand to the north, its heartland is a fertile plain as flat as a calm sea. The Thais are a different race from the Malays; in fact, they are closer to the Chinese in

1

appearance, distinguishable from the Malays by their lighter skins and their almond-shaped eyes. Almost all of them are Buddhists.

Uniquely in ASEAN, Thailand was never colonized by a foreign power. By a mixture of luck, timely internal reform and skilful diplomacy, it managed to keep itself free of the European empires that carved up the region among themselves in the 19th century. The old, absolutist kingdom of Siam has now become a constitutional monarchy—although, as in Indonesia, the army plays a key political role.

Like a gently angled kris—the wavy-bladed Malay sword—West Malaysia descends below Thailand and points straight into the Java Sea. The only land link between the Indonesian archipelago and the Indochinese mainland, the Malaysian federation also reaches 700 kilometres across the South China Sea to include East Malaysia—the states of Sabah and Sarawak on the northern part of Borneo, which between them make up 60 per cent of the country.

Malaysia used to be a British colony; West Malaysia, previously known as Malaya, gained its independence in 1957, the Borneo lands in 1963. Today, Malaysia is a democracy that has a curious kind of revolving monarchy: each of Malaysia's nine hereditary sultans holds office in turn for a five-year period.

A century ago, most of the population of Malaysia was Malay and Muslim. But now the Malays make up only 47 per cent of the total population of 15 million, thanks to large numbers of Chinese and Indians introduced to develop the economy by the British. The large Chinese minority is heavily represented in the modernized, urban

A Javanese woman in a traditional skirt-like sarong shelters from a downpour as she waits for a rickshaw. Monsoon winds bring heavy rain to much of South-East Asia; nearly 2,000 millimetres fall annually on Java.

sector of the economy. Disparities in wealth and power cause some tension between Malay and Chinese communities—communal riots in 1969 claimed more than 200 lives—but a spirit of compromise generally prevails.

Impressive natural resources and a steadily growing manufacturing base have helped to give Malaysia a relatively high standard of living. Thailand, the Philippines and Indonesia are all rated by the World Bank as "lower-middle income" countries, and Malaysia has graduated to "upper-middle income" status.

But the region's greatest economic success story is its smallest state, the island-city of Singapore. Built from scratch by the British in 1819, Singapore and its predominantly Chinese population went their independent way in 1965. Since then, the city-state has surged ahead under the authoritarian but elected rule of Lee Kuan Yew and his People's Action Party. Its average annual economic growth rate from 1960 to 1982 of 7.4 per cent was not only one of the highest in the world; it also lifted Singapore's per capita GNP to $5,910 by 1982—higher than those of Spain and Greece.

Singapore's 2.5 million people grumble at Lee's sometimes heavy-handed ways—a speech in which he urged women university graduates to have more children, with a view to increasing the average IQ of the island's population, was widely ridiculed—but there is little real dissent. The small republic is too proud of its record, its high-technology skills and its reputation as the most dynamic city in Asia.

The countries of South-East Asia, different as they are from one another, also embrace a great deal of internal diversity. The Malay populations of Indonesia and the Philippines are far from homogeneous: over the centuries, they have fragmented into numerous societies, each with their own cultural traditions and languages. These two countries and Malaysia also house many communities of tribal peoples. Thailand is culturally more unified, but its mountains shelter a number of racial minorities: mainly semi-nomadic peoples who have migrated in the past hundred years from farther north. Everywhere except in the miniature state of Singapore, the contrasts between cities and countryside are astonishing. The ASEAN capitals are as sophisticated and cosmopolitan as any in the world, yet not far away live farmers, fishermen and hunter-gatherers whose lives have hardly been touched by the 20th century.

It was never the intention that ASEAN should forge a single unit from the diversity of South-East Asia, and if it tried it would certainly fail. It has, however, allowed its members to know and understand one another. Regular meetings, standing committees and frequent cultural exchanges have all contributed to the slow but steady growth of a regional identity. ASEAN is a framework for peace and stability—no more, perhaps, but certainly no less. It was largely for the sense of security which ASEAN membership provides that Brunei, the tiny, oil-rich statelet in northern Borneo, joined when it became independent of Britain in 1984. It was much colder outside.

As Singapore's Lee Kuan Yew put it at a 1983 meeting, ASEAN has reached the point of *musyawarah*—a carefully chosen Indonesian word that means something like "the dialogue leading to consensus". For all their differences, the peoples of South-East Asia share a deep-felt desire for a common position. From the level of a simple village meeting to the level of government policy-making, South-East Asians would rather reach some sort of general agreement, however long discussions may take, than press their own ideas on others by force or indeed by simple majority voting. This feature running through the region's societies helps stabilize them in the face of internal upheavals and now is a key factor in promoting harmony within ASEAN.

All of the ASEAN governments, however authoritarian or democratic, reflect the tendency towards consensus. Malaysia's parliamentary democracy has, ever since Independence, produced a coalition government that represents all three of the country's main political parties, while military

During a Hindu festival on Bali, shrines with symbolic coloured cloths fill a temple enclosure. Unlike the rest of Indonesia, which had largely converted to Islam by the 16th century, Bali has remained a stronghold of the older faith, celebrating religious holidays with splendid ritual.

1

regimes in Thailand succeed one another with scarcely any of the bloodshed and destruction seen in so many African and South American countries. But while the desire for consensus generally damps down conflict, it does occasionally have its darker side. If the status quo is threatened by a force that cannot be incorporated into the framework of agreement, violence of the most savage kind can erupt. Such was the case in Indonesia in 1965. After the Communists failed to seize power, they perished by the hundred thousand in reprisals.

The desire for consensus did not spring out of thin air: it is reinforced by the whole way of life of the region, which in turn is consequent on the climate. Very high rainfall makes rice an ideal crop, and the most productive method of rice cultivation requires a joint effort from an entire village. The outcome of centuries of teamwork is a society in which everyone functions, willingly enough, within fairly tight conventions; there is a strong sense of mutual obligation—and an equally strong sense of shame if obligations are not met—combined with deference to authority and deep mistrust of change.

The climate is remarkably similar everywhere in South-East Asia: the temperature remains very close to 28°C throughout the year and a heavy monsoon rainfall spreads itself over at least six months. In the latter part of the year, many places within the region experience torrential downpours almost every day.

Rice thrives on the heat and the abundant rain and it is the cultivation of rice that occupies most of South-East Asia's farmers—who in 1980 made up 76 per cent of the population in Thailand, 58 per cent in Indonesia, 50 per cent in Malaysia and 46 per cent in the Philippines. Therefore, although agriculture is no longer the main source of income, it is still by far the biggest employer everywhere except in

urban Singapore. It remains, as it always has been, the great shaper of culture and outlook.

Rice has an almost mystical importance in South-East Asia, where it has provided the great bulk of everyday nourishment for thousands of years. Most people eat very little else: a few drops of palm or coconut oil, some vegetables or chillies for flavouring, and—if they can afford it—a few fragments of fish for protein. (According to one Thai legend, when the universe was young, rice alone was sufficient. But with the steady increase in evil since those far-off beginnings, other flavourings have become a regrettable necessity.) Through its predominance, rice has come to be seen as more than mere provender; it represents well-being and even honour. Thus, to maintain one's self-respect and the respect of one's neighbours, three meals of white rice every day are, culturally speaking, mandatory; and it would be deeply shameful not to have a store of rice in the house at all times.

The remarkable grain can flourish in virtually every variant of South-East Asian geography. There are three methods of rice cultivation and at least one of them will suit most terrains. The first is shifting cultivation, or "slash-and-burn". Surprising though it is nowadays to think of rice growing in the forest, slash-and-burn is by far the oldest way of growing the cereal; the relative importance of slash-and-burn may have diminished but it is still practised in sparsely populated regions, especially by tribal minorities.

The technique is rudimentary. A village group simply cuts down a few hectares of forest, allows the dead wood to dry for a few months, and burns it. In the nutrient-rich ash, they plant their rice. After harvest, they move elsewhere for the next crop and allow the forest to return to its natural state. The method has considerable advantages: scarcely any equipment is required and a modest amount of labour can yield a handsome return. But shifting cultivation has one great drawback: since the forest requires at least nine years to regenerate itself, the method requires a lot of land. Should the population increase, and some farmers be tempted to shorten the fallow interval, the result is always the same. The fragile rainforest soil loses nutrients faster than they can be replaced, yields fall disastrously, the farmers starve and the forest ecology is ruined for years to come, perhaps for ever.

The second method—broadcasting, or dry cultivation—uses fixed fields and necessitates ploughing. It probably began when local population pressures started to make slash-and-burn impracticable. Large areas may be cleared—provided they are in river valleys, or at any rate receive floodwaters—and in the dry season they are ploughed and seeded with deep-rooted rice varieties. The land itself is not the source of the rice plants' nourishment. That comes instead from the rising floods of the rainy season, because the waters that inundate the fields are rich in nutrients washed from upland forest soil. At the expense of the draught animals and equipment which shifting cultivators do not need, the method guarantees a higher yield from a given area of land.

Dry cultivation, historically important, is now practised only in confined pockets. In most of South-East Asia, a third method—transplanting, or wet-rice cultivation—has long been the norm. Rice seedlings are cultivated in nursery beds and then transplanted into fields and kept under water to just the right level. Water control is essential, whether it involves no more than carefully maintained dykes round a field to hold seasonal rainfalls, or enormously complex irrigation schemes designed to tap and tame the floodwaters of a major river system. The labour costs of transplanting individual seedlings by hand are immense, especially in Java and parts of the Philippines, where water-retaining terraces ascend mountains almost to the clouds. But the benefits of wet-rice cultivation are also huge. Dykes give the cultivators the control that dry-rice farmers lack and, if the land is irrigated with a year-round supply of river water, wet-rice cultivation allows two or three crops in a year. Where the terrain is suitable, the method can support far higher populations than the earlier-evolved methods—sometimes more than 400 people for each square kilometre.

As well as labour, however, wet-rice cultivation demands a very high degree of social co-operation. Not only is the initial investment of energy and materials in terracing, dyking and ditching far beyond the resources of any one family group or even a small village, but the maintenance required at all times and the special efforts needed at specific moments in the annual cycle—transplanting and harvesting, for example—would be impossible without wholehearted agreement and application: without, in a word, consensus. Although wet-rice cultivation is vastly more efficient than the ancient slash-and-burn method in terms of the population it can support, it is also vastly more fragile. It depends upon a pattern of human symbiosis much more intricate even than the

A pepper plantation cuts a swathe through the dense jungle of Kalimantan—the Indonesian part of Borneo. Indonesia is the world's third largest supplier of pepper, a spice that has drawn Europeans to South-East Asia since the 16th century.

23

1

highly complex systems of water engineering which are its outward signs.

The traditions of consensus that wet-rice farming made imperative are reinforced by religious beliefs. Both Islam and Thai Buddhism put strong emphasis on the community. Religious festivals remind villagers of their common needs and goals.

At the village level, South-East Asia works in a reasonably egalitarian way, with an emphasis on politeness and consideration for others. Villagers traditionally collaborate for house building, support the sick and unemployed in their community, and share any windfalls as well as the consequences of a bad harvest.

But the push towards consensus is anything but democratic in the Western sense; indeed, it operates largely by respect for authority. In a village meeting, for instance, everyone's concurrence in a decision will certainly be sought; but in practice no ordinary peasant is likely to raise his voice against the headman. Even the Communist Party, when it was actively recruiting in Indonesian villages in the 1950s and 1960s, could not make any headway against traditional patterns of respect—although it did turn them to its advantage. Instead of stirring up class feeling among the individual villagers, they went straight to the headman. If they could impress him by their policies, they knew he would bring his village into the Party fold.

Throughout South-East Asia, headmen are elected—after a fashion—by their fellow-villagers. That is, only a man of standing, usually relatively wealthy, will be selected; he will invariably be able to rely on the support of all those who work for him or have incurred some other obligation, and the election is likely to be uncontested. In fact, rather than call the process an election at all, it might be better to say simply that the headman is chosen after a period of discussion.

In spite of the ingrained conservatism of South-East Asia, the role of the village headman is changing. In the past, particularly during the colonial period, the headman was very much the representative of the villagers to higher authority. He would receive visitors from the outside world and, if necessary, journey to town to confer with the provincial authorities. Nowadays, however, his role is more the representative of government to the villagers—an unpaid civil servant. He is expected to collect taxes on behalf of the central government and to organize military conscription.

That is only one example of the changes that are coming increasingly quickly to a change-resistant society. Change is most obvious in the cities, of course, with their new industries, their skyscrapers, their bustle—and their astonishing growth. Each of the region's three largest cities—Bangkok, Manila and Jakarta—is fast becoming a megalopolis. According to current projections, the 16.6 million people who are expected to live in Jakarta by the year 2000 will make it the world's 10th largest city. About 10 per cent of Thailand's population live in Bangkok; an even larger proportion of the Philippines' population live in Manila.

But change is at work in the countryside too, less obviously but more importantly, because that is where most South-East Asians live. Much rural change has been the result of the so-called Green Revolution—the package of improved crop strains, new farming techniques and modern equipment that is transforming large parts of the developing world. The improvements it has brought have allowed a general increase in prosperity and more to eat for everybody, but there have been profound cultural effects as well. The rich have benefited most, since it is they who have money to invest in fertilizer and equipment; the differentials between successful and unsuccessful farmers are wider than ever. Success, in turn, breeds a certain capitalist turn of mind, which runs directly against traditions of consensus.

In Java, for example, villagers used to harvest rice with old-fashioned, inefficient knives that left a sizeable proportion of grain behind. It was not wasted: its gleaning served as payment for the local landless poor who had helped with the harvest. Now, farmers use better and more costly equipment that clears the fields efficiently, suiting its more money-conscious owners but weakening the ties of mutual support that bind the village together. Indeed, a prosperous farmer will often use workers from another village 30 kilometres or more away, who will be paid in a straightforward and contractual fashion with none of the complex social obligations that would be incurred were he to recruit his field hands from among his neighbours.

Yet the old ways are not going to vanish overnight. Deference, politeness, the desire for agreement, are profoundly embedded in cultures as superficially different as Buddhist Thailand, the Christian Philippines and Muslim Indonesia. The traits come from the land itself, and the manner by which, for centuries, it has been worked. They are native in a way that even the great faiths that have entrenched themselves in the area are

THE SULTANATE OF OIL

The pocket-sized state of Brunei, composed of two adjacent enclaves on Borneo's northern coast, is awash with oil. Thanks to the petroleum and natural gas that account for 99 per cent of its exports, Brunei's gross domestic product per head is the third highest in the world.

Most of the wealth is at the personal disposal of the Sultan—the last of Asia's absolute rulers—who lives in luxury in a 1,788-room palace. But he has invested some of the oil revenue in excellent health-care and schooling to benefit the populace at large.

Malays—most of whom work the land—make up two thirds of the state's 200,000 population. A further 30 per cent are ethnic Chinese, who dominate business life. Their status is precarious, however, for Brunei is strongly Islamic and most non-Muslims are denied citizenship.

Brunei converted to Islam in the 15th century. For a time thereafter, Brunei ruled much of Borneo, but later its power declined and in 1888 it became a British protectorate. Already an oil-producer in 1963 when Britain's other Borneo lands fused with Malaya, Brunei chose to retain the colonial link rather than dilute its prosperity as part of the new nation. It finally became independent in 1984.

The glittering dome of a modern mosque towers over the watery heart of Brunei's capital, Bandar Seri Begawan.

1

not. The Indonesians—who call the whole complex code of customary behaviour by the deceptively short word *adat*—have a saying which acknowledges this truth: "Religion comes in from the sea, but *adat* comes down from the mountains."

The first half of that Indonesian proverb has almost as much significance as the second. The sea has made a crucial impact on the societies of the area.

Three of the ASEAN countries are island states and the others all have extensive coastlines. The Chinese have long recognized the significance of this: their name for what the West calls South-East Asia, Nan Yang, translates literally as "the South Sea". Within South-East Asia, the sea is the natural route between communities, fish a major resource, boatmanship universal. And because of the area's position at the maritime crossroads where the

Indian and the Pacific Oceans meet, it has for centuries been one of the most cosmopolitan places in the world.

The ocean highways brought traders, and with the trade inevitably came ideas. The earliest foreign precepts notably to influence the region came from India in the form of Hinduism and Buddhism—but, like everything else that came to South-East Asia, both of them were adapted to suit the needs of local societies. Hinduism, for instance, arrived almost 2,000 years ago and spread rapidly over most of the region; but although its people accepted the Hindu pantheon—as well as the skilled administrative services of the Indian Brahmins who proselytized the new religion—they never adopted the rigid caste system that stratifies Indian society. Today, the Hindu heritage is apparent in the rituals of the Malaysian and Thai courts and in the folklore and dramatic arts of the entire region. However, other more aggressive faiths have long since won away most of the religion's adherents. Only in the Indonesian island of Bali is it still widely practised. Even there, it is very different from the Indian version: one of the foremost ways for an Indian Hindu to practise his religion is to follow minutely his particular caste's rules for daily life, whereas the Balinese, lacking India's division into castes, are much less constricted.

Similarly, Buddhism, which spread from India in the seventh century, underwent a few sea-changes before it developed into Thailand's national religion. Today, it coexists there with indigenous religious practices, such as the veneration of the Rice Mother: the spirit of the grain.

India's contribution to South-East Asian culture was always qualified by strong trading links with China, but the next cultural influence to rock the region dramatically came not from the north but from far to the west. The confident message of Islam was brought by Arab merchants to coastal communities in South-East Asia as early as 1250. It took firm root in the 15th century with the conversion of the ruler of Malacca, a mighty though short-lived empire extending over Malaya and a good part of Sumatra. In the next two centuries, Islam spread outwards from the Malay peninsula, supported by Malaccan power and carried by Malaccan ships throughout the South-East Asian archipelago as far as Mindanao, now in the southern Philippines. Islam made only limited headway in Buddhist Thailand and its neighbours, but almost everywhere else it was accepted with enthusiasm.

It still is. Perhaps Islam's fiery simplicity appealed to men and women tired of the hierarchic Hindu worldview; perhaps its profound fatalism struck a chord with tropical peoples noted then as now for their cheerful insouciance. At any rate, present-day Indonesia has the world's largest Muslim population, while Islam is in the Malaysian Constitution: to be a Malay in Malaysia is, officially, to be a Muslim. Brunei, too, is solidly Islamic, and all the other countries have Muslim minorities, often substantial.

Islam in South-East Asia is rarely the fiercely intolerant, fire-and-sword faith of the Arabian Peninsula. Like Hinduism and Buddhism before it, it has been "tropicalized" into something a good deal gentler and more easy-going. Extremists do exist, however. During Indonesia's struggle to gain independence, a movement called Darul Islam—literally, "The House of Islam"—took up arms to establish an Islamic state. It was put down but never eliminated completely. In the Philippines, too, militant Islam sometimes adds to the government's security problems. And in Malaysia, which apart from Brunei is the most orthodox Muslim country of South-East Asia, fundamentalism is growing. But most South-East Asians—though certainly devout, as the large numbers who make a pilgrimage to Mecca attest—are simply not single-minded enough to make good fanatics.

Less than a hundred years after Islam reached South-East Asia, the Europeans arrived. They were drawn initially by the immensely lucrative spice trade but they stayed to build empires: the boundaries of the modern nations of South-East Asia result from the caprice and design of competing European powers. Each imperial ruler placed its own distinctive mark on the territory under its sway.

The Portuguese were the first Europeans on the scene. They were soon ousted by the Dutch from most of their trading stations but they retained a solitary foothold—East Timor, in the Indonesian archipelago—right up until 1975, thus becoming the last colonial power to leave South-East Asia.

Even before the Dutch arrived, the Spanish had set about annexing the Philippines. Unlike the other European intruders, they attempted—and achieved—wholesale conversion of the natives to their religion. To this day, 85 per cent of Filipinos are Catholics. The Spaniards also gave the Philippines their name, in honour of their king, Philip II.

At the end of the 18th century, the British established a foothold on an island off the Malay Peninsula and subsequently expanded their influence. In the course of the following century, they came to control most of what would become Malaysia, Singapore and Brunei; the Dutch established their hold on Indonesia and the Spanish remained firmly ensconced in the Philippines. Among the ASEAN countries, only Thailand managed to retain its independence.

The European colonizers controlling most of the region began, towards the end of the 19th century, systematically to exploit the region's resources. They introduced new crops and employed unfamiliar agricultural methods to create the most lucrative plantation economies the world has ever seen. Only they had the funds to clear whole sections of forest, replant scientifically, and then endure the profitless years until the new trees were old enough to yield. Their efforts changed the face of South-East Asia and had repercussions that are still being felt today.

Although spices had drawn the Europeans to the area initially, tobacco, sugar and coffee had overtaken them in value by the late 19th century, and two extraneous crops had joined the region's native mainstays. One was the oil palm, a native of West Africa, whose fruit yields oil for margarine and soap. The Dutch had introduced it into Sumatra on an experimental basis as early as 1848, but it was many years before demand for the crop's derivatives built up to a spectacular level. The other novelty, rubber, took off much more rapidly.

Rubber trees originally grew wild in Brazil's Amazon jungle, and until the late 19th century supply of the small quantities used by the world's markets was a Brazilian monopoly. But in 1876 an enterprising British botanist smuggled seeds to England, where they were germinated in the Royal Botanic Gardens at Kew, near London. Seedlings were sent to Ceylon and to Singapore, reaching Malaya in the 1890s—to coincide with the arrival of the new automobile industry in Europe and the U.S. Production of pneumatic tyres sent demand for the commodity spiralling upwards. Within a decade, rubber was Malaya's most valuable export, while rubber trees were being planted in Java, Sumatra, Borneo: anywhere they could be made to grow.

The prime sites for plantations were in almost every case thinly populated. In Malaysia the self-sufficient peasant smallholders had no desire to uproot themselves in order to work on the plantations, and the British preferred

A merchant of the Dutch East India Company, hand in hand with his wife, points proudly to company ships at Batavia (now Jakarta) in the 1640s.

not to interfere with their traditional societies. The Dutch partially solved the problem of the labour shortage in Sumatra by transplanting Malays from crowded Java. The shortfall elsewhere was made up by importing workers from afar. The British shipped Indians by the million to labour in Malaysia; British and Dutch alike opened their ports to a flood of Chinese. Unwittingly—or at any rate unconcernedly—the Western developers had precipitated one of history's great migrations, comparable to the movement of European peoples across the Atlantic to the United States.

Many of the newcomers came only as contracted labourers, pledged to return to their homelands with their meagre savings after a few years' work, but millions stayed. The inevitable racial tensions were exacerbated by the fact that the Asian middle class which emerged in the colonial period—managers and under-managers, and not a few extremely prosperous merchants and ship-owners—tended to be recruited from the immigrant Chinese and Indian communities.

Imperialist energy and the new racial leavening undoubtedly worked economic wonders. By the 1930s, as a whole, South-East Asia was providing the bulk of the tropical produce bought and sold on the world's markets: 93 per cent of the rubber, for example, 75 per cent of the copra and 55 per cent of the palm oil. Malaya alone yielded 60 per cent of the world's tin.

But colonial development had its drawbacks. The main one, from the point of view of the colonized countries, was that most of the wealth produced disappeared into the coffers of the imperial powers. Part of it went into improving health care and sanitation throughout the region, which caused a marked rise in life expectancy; wages, however, remained distressingly low. Moreover, the emphasis on exports led to economies that were rich in parts and entirely neglected in others.

Everywhere, the educated élite came to resent the imposition of foreign

Palms front Cebu City's cathedral, one of many baroque churches built by the Spanish during their 300-year rule over the Philippines.

Neatly dressed in their school uniform, young Singaporean girls smile self-consciously for a group photograph. In the post-Independence era, all of the South-East Asian countries strove to provide universal primary education; Singapore achieved the goal first, in the late 1960s.

rule and to envy the rulers their opportunities. In the fast-growing and half-modern cities of the early 20th century, nationalism was in the air.

The currents were felt among the new administrative class even in Thailand, which had never been colonized. Trained to serve faithfully as the stewards of an enlightened despot, the bureaucrats grew jealous of their king's absolute power. The result was a coup in 1932 which constitutionalized the absolute monarchy.

The nationalists elsewhere had their chance, too, far sooner than they had expected. The Japanese onslaught in World War II swept Western rule from South-East Asia in six brief months, boosting Asian morale and destroying European prestige. Most nationalists welcomed the changeover and collaborated with the Japanese, who in return granted many of them limited self-government and even raised small local armies. Although it became clear that Japanese rule was just as oppressive and far more brutal than the European dominion it had replaced, it did give nationalists a taste of power. When Japan's short-lived Greater East Asian Co-Prosperity Sphere collapsed in turn in 1945, it was clear that there could be no return to the pre-war status quo. Over the next two decades, the territories which later became ASEAN members were all granted their own independence.

Since the war, all of the ASEAN countries have had to face similar problems. All had economies designed to supply the needs of far-off Western markets. All had a serious shortage of trained personnel, especially scientists, technologists and engineers. All had to accommodate racial minorities, some

of substantial size. All had to face a tide of rising expectations among their populations, and the likelihood of dangerous political problems if these expectations remained unfulfilled—the more so since within the area only Thailand could rely on a long tradition of national cohesion. Most of these problems were the result of colonialist policies. They have all had to be dealt with in the teeth of fast-rising populations—the outcome of the successful reduction of death rates achieved during the colonial era.

Compared with most of the Third World, ASEAN has done well. Indeed, from the mid-1970s to the mid 1980s, it grew faster than any other group of developing countries. All the ASEAN nations except Brunei have established some manufacturing capability: Brunei is still entirely import-dependent for its basic requirements, but with

an oil-boosted per capita income of $21,000 a year, its people can afford them. Many of the region's industries are joint ventures with foreign multinational corporations, usually either American or Japanese: car plants in Thailand and the Philippines, for instance, or tyre production in Indonesia. Malaysia has a major vehicle plant—the federation has made efforts to reduce the influence of Western and Japanese capital on its economy—and also produces a significant proportion of the world's computer microchips. Singapore will build anything that fits on to its busy little island.

For the time being, however, minerals and commodity crops remain crucial. Five of the six ASEAN member nations still rely heavily on minerals and other primary products for the bulk of their exports, while the sixth—Singapore—depends on trading them.

For Malaysia, the rubber and tin that kept the British Empire solvent are no longer so important; their prime position has been taken by oil, timber and palm oil. Indonesia has the same range of commodities as well as the fertile, volcanic soils of Java. The Philippines are blessed with copper and gold. Thailand has its fertile Chao Phraya delta and is developing an offshore gas field in the Gulf of Thailand.

In every country there has been a serious effort to develop the most basic resource of all: the people. By the 1980s, primary education was virtually universal in all the ASEAN countries except Thailand, while secondary enrolments ranged from 29 per cent in Thailand to 65 per cent in Singapore.

Education, however, has not been an unrelieved blessing, especially at the higher levels. Only a fraction of the students choking the big universities and institutes of learning in such cities as Bangkok and Manila will qualify in much-needed technological skills. The rest will have to be accommodated in the bureaucracies, or settle for menial jobs or even unemployment, where their disappointment could turn to dangerous discontent.

Of all South-East Asia's various peoples, none is more passionate about education than the Chinese. They themselves should probably be seen as one of the region's most valuable resources. Dynamic, entrepreneurial and everywhere distrusted, they control a hugely disproportionate share of regional trade and industry—where they are not specifically excluded from it by legislation. They are active in all the professions, are generally better-off than their South-East Asian neighbours (though many Chinese, however, are abysmally poor), and they are

JAPAN'S WAR OF CONQUEST

Within hours of entering World War II on December 7, 1941, Japan launched an all-out assault on South-East Asia. Surprise air attacks on the Philippines and Singapore were followed by an almost unopposed invasion of Malaya and then of Singapore, which surrendered in February 1942. Troops also landed in the Dutch East Indies and the Philippines, which fell after brave resistance on March 9 and April 9 respectively. After an offensive of just 122 days, the Japanese were masters of the entire region.

Except in Singapore, where air raids killed hundreds of people from all races, few civilians in South-East Asia were scarred by Japan's lightning strike. But the three-year Japanese occupation that followed brought a heavy toll of suffering. While Europeans were herded into prison camps and forced labour, Japanese secret police terrorized local populations, and economic chaos caused many to starve.

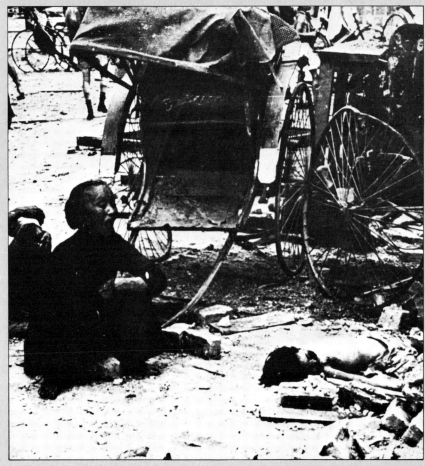

A Singaporean mother grieves over her child, killed in a Japanese air raid.

feared as well as respected for their commercial acumen.

They are scattered throughout the region and, because they almost invariably live in the big cities, they give the impression to the traveller of being more numerous than they are. Their numbers in fact range from 3 per cent of the population of Indonesia, about 8 per cent in Thailand, 28 per cent in Brunei and 35 per cent in Malaysia to 76 per cent of that of Singapore. In the Philippines, less than 2 per cent of the population is of pure Chinese stock but the proportion with some Chinese blood is much higher.

The legal status of the Chinese varies from country to country, from the full citizenship extended to them—a little grudgingly—in Malaysia to the state of official non-existence in which they live in Brunei, where only Muslims are citizens. The Chinese occupy a position, in fact, much like that of Europe's Jews throughout most of European history: a people accused of clannishness, suspected of alien loyalties and frequently blamed for every misfortune, as well as being creative, industrious and almost indispensable. In Thailand and the Philippines, intermarriage is helping to integrate them, but mixed marriages are virtually unknown in the Muslim societies of Malaysia and Indonesia.

The dominant role of the Chinese in trade and commerce is beginning to diminish now, not only because of laws in most countries that limit their participation, but because Malays, Thais, Filipinos and Indonesians are learning the traditional Chinese skills themselves. The proportion of Chinese in the population at large is likely to shrink as well, simply because of their relatively low birth rate: as a group,

the Chinese community has already crossed over the threshold into the relative affluence which acts as a brake upon fertility.

In most of South-East Asia, though, the pressure of rising populations is still a serious problem. Once again, Indonesia provides the most dramatic example. A 1905 census counted 38 million people in the area of today's nation; there were over 80 million by the 1950s, 153 million in 1982 and it is estimated that there will be 212 million by the year 2000. The graphs for Thailand and the Philippines are almost as steep. Space in these three countries is becoming scarce, though Malaysia has room to spare.

The population problem is one that the region's governments take very seriously indeed. Most are engaged in sophisticated family planning campaigns, and in addition Indonesia runs a programme of assisted resettlement from grossly overcrowded Java to outlying islands where there is empty land. Rising prosperity—in demographic terms the most effective contraceptive of all—is beginning to have an effect. But, except in Singapore, the falling birth rates have not yet dropped enough to match falling death rates.

In a sense, the ASEAN countries are engaged in a race to get rich before their surging populations condemn them to poverty. Given the enterprise of their people, the economic growth they have so far achieved and the growing harmony in the region, the prospects seem bright. ASEAN will not of itself promote the growth its members need. But ASEAN's existence does allow its members to pursue their own policies in peace. Lee Kuan Yew's "dialogue leading to consensus" is well under way.

A mission helicopter draws curious onlookers from their huts among the misty highlands of Irian Jaya, Indonesia's easternmost territory. Until air contact was established in the past few decades, many Irianese lived a secluded stone-age existence.

An offering at a Balinese festival,
featuring the head of the Hindu demon
Bhoma, serves to ward off the spirit's
evil presence. Made entirely of vividly
coloured rice dough, the offering
stands taller than a man; it typifies
Indonesian art in its swirling lines
and intricate detail.

A REPUBLIC OF ISLANDS

The world's sixth largest and fifth most populous nation is no older than a bold proclamation willing it into existence on August 17, 1945. The Republic of Indonesia's Declaration of Independence signalled the end of more than three centuries of Dutch dominion, but it took four years of warfare before the Dutch reluctantly agreed to leave the country. In December 1949, Indonesian sovereignty became a reality.

A major geopolitical power had been created. Its essential stability, in contrast with so many newly emerging countries, is attested by the tally of its presidents: only two, in more than 40 years of independence. Today, large foreign embassy staffs closely monitor the international relations of the capital Jakarta, one of Asia's strategic centres. Multinational corporations invest billions of dollars in an economy that boasts an impressive range of resources, including the largest known oil and gas reserves in non-Communist Asia. Nearby Malaysia and Brunei acknowledge their enormous neighbour as both the cultural and political pivot of the Malay world.

It would have taken a bold seer to predict today's confident role for Indonesia at the time of Independence, because the country hardly looked like a natural political unit. It is made up of 13,677 islands strewn across more than 5,000 kilometres of tropical seas—a spread that exceeds the distance from California to Florida and from Ireland to eastern Turkey. Many of these islands are no more than rocky outcrops, and only 8 per cent of them are per-manently inhabited, but that small proportion includes most of Borneo, the world's third largest island, and half of New Guinea, the second largest.

The galaxy of islands encompasses endless diversity. The climate is wettest in the west and some of the eastern islands are quite arid. And the vegetation changes accordingly, from the dense rainforest of Kalimantan—Indonesian Borneo—to the dusty savannahs of Timor. Racially, too, there is a progression with longitude. In the western islands, most people have the brown skin, straight hair and clear-cut features of the typical Malay. Towards the east, most notably in Irian Jaya—western New Guinea—many have the tightly curled hair, dark skin and blunter features of the Melanesians, a group scattered across the South Pacific. Within these two broad categories there is a complex mosaic of ethnic types. A vast array of traditional and modern lifestyles and 250 distinct languages compound the variety.

Superficially, Indonesia's diverse and scattered peoples might appear to have little in common beyond the experience of having been ruled by the Dutch. The limits of the Dutch possession certainly determined the parameters of Indonesia, but the country is far from an artificial creation. The islands had a long history of contact with each other; among the coastal peoples, in particular, a high coincidence of custom and ritual had developed. A succession of empires based in Java and Sumatra had extended their influence over other parts of the archipelago. After the advent of Islam from the 13th century onwards, religion became a powerful bond. Despite the survival of many animist and mystical beliefs, nearly 90 per cent of Indonesians follow Islam, giving the country by far the largest population of Muslims in the world today.

The Dutch strengthened these tentative bonds by imposing an administrative unity on the archipelago. They also contributed in a more negative way to the nationalist cause: by providing a common focus for resentment, they drew the islanders together.

The Javanese have long been the most numerous of Indonesia's populations, and they were prominent in the Independence movement that gathered strength in the 1920s and 1930s. Had they tried to impose a specifically Javanese stamp on the movement, they might easily have caused a rift which would have split Indonesia into two or more countries. But they were wise enough not to antagonize other islanders. They refrained, for example, from promoting their own language. Javanese would, in any case, have been unsuitable for a modern nation. Developed in the hierarchic world of the Javanese courts, it employs three distinct vocabularies which allow the speaker to define his social status as superior, equal or inferior to the listener.

Seeking a more egalitarian means of communication, the nationalists hit upon "market Malay", which had been the lingua franca of traders and sailors throughout the archipelago for centuries. The language was unsullied

2

by status consciousness and acceptable to all Indonesians because it was linked to none in particular. Now called *bahasa Indonesia*—the Indonesian language—the tongue is the envy of other large and heterogeneous countries such as India. It is the language of officialdom and the means of instruction in all secondary schools; it dominates the media and the streets of the principal cities. In their villages people continue to speak their own languages but everyone has a knowledge of Indonesian.

With a common language to help strengthen the glue of a joint colonial past and a religion shared by the vast majority, Indonesia has achieved a powerful sense of nationhood. The sentiment is not quite universal, however. In Irian Jaya and East Timor—two latecomers which were coerced into Indonesia in 1963 and 1975 respectively, widespread resentment of the annexations still finds expression in simmering guerrilla conflict. But elsewhere, secessionist movements are virtually non-existent. The nation can display with justification its motto, "Unity in Diversity".

A tour of Indonesia's ample sweep begins most naturally near the core—the so-called "inner islands" of Java, Bali and Lombok, which possess the most spectacularly fertile soils in the world. They owe their lushness to regular monsoon rains and to a chain of volcanoes stretching along their length. Many of the volcanoes are active and, though their eruptions occasionally bring disaster on an awesome scale, they also have a kindly effect: their grey ash, full of chemical nutrients, enriches the surrounding soil to such an extent that even wooden fence-posts

MERDEKA!
INDONESIAKU

A poster commemorating Indonesia's Declaration of Independence from the Dutch in 1945 portrays the two leading campaigners for freedom, Sukarno *(left)* and Hatta *(right)*. They became Indonesia's first president and vice president respectively.

sometimes sprout into an impenetrable thicket within a couple of years.

All three islands grow rice crops intensively and the ordered landscapes that result, especially in the small but varied compass of Bali, are reminiscent of a lovingly tended garden. In some places the flooded paddy fields reflect the azure sky; elsewhere the land is a patchwork of greens, as adjacent plots ripen a day or two apart. On steep slopes, mountains are terraced into giant, curving steeps above which emerge the imposing volcanic peaks.

With their extraordinary fertility, the inner islands can support a vast multitude. A staggering 100 million people live on Java, a territory about the same size as England. Its population accounts for nearly two thirds of all Indonesians and one third of the entire population of ASEAN. The numerical weighting of the Javanese regularly brings them to the fore in Indonesian life. Java also has historical claims to pre-eminence as the focal point of the early kingdoms whose courtly culture has now become In-

donesia's national heritage. Later, Java became the main base of the Dutch.

The Dutch political headquarters, Batavia, on Java's north shore, is now the capital Jakarta, a city which, according to predictions, will be one of the largest in the world by the 21st century. Despite attempts in the 1970s to close Jakarta to newcomers, it still acts as a magnet for rural migrants, who could swell today's population of eight to nine million to 20 million by the year 2000. No one—not even the city government—knows how many people actually live in the sprawl of red-tiled houses that stretches from the mouth of the heavily polluted Ciliwung river to the exclusive housing estates raised by speculators along the former paddy fields at the city's southern edge.

For the lucky few, there are all the diversions that money and influence can procure. Four-star hotels line the main Jalan Thamrin boulevard. Golf clubs, amusement centres and luxury-goods shops dot the wealthy southern suburbs. Oil money has created a subclass of *nouveaux riches* who often shop in Singapore at weekends and travel to Amsterdam four or five times a year. Wealthy Chinese businessmen live in splendour, albeit behind closed doors, and the pampered children of top government officials and army personnel go to school in chauffeur-driven cars that speed down the new highways cutting across the city.

About a third of Jakarta's citizens, however, live in desperate poverty in squalid squatter communities that lack virtually all amenities. Some of these settlements are of such long standing that two generations have grown up in their earthen-floored huts jammed into shallow recesses between the larger commercial developments.

In Jakarta, capital of Indonesia, a broad avenue cuts through an infinity of modest, red-tiled buildings—many of them the homes and workplaces of small tradesmen. With few high-rise blocks, Jakarta retains the atmosphere of an overgrown village despite its population of more than eight million.

Most of their inhabitants live a hand-to-mouth existence by peddling cigarettes, shining shoes or scavenging.

With all life spilling into the streets, Jakarta's frenzy never pauses. In the narrow streets, three-wheeled taxis, motorcycles, badly dented buses and pedi-cabs jostling for custom create a perpetual cacophany, while at night one enclave or another is sure to offer a comic street spectacle to celebrate a local boy's circumcision or a wedding.

For all Jakarta's frenetic rate of growth, two thirds of Java's inhabitants are still rural folk—fishermen putting to sea in lateen-rigged outriggers or peasants setting out at four in the morning to their rice fields. Their villages typically comprise a collection of bamboo and palm-leaf houses, many within tiny courtyards. Here, life still moves to the rhythm of the soil—the cycle of planting, irrigating, draining, harvesting and threshing.

But the tempo is quickening even in Java's rural heartland. New roads, inexpensive motorcycles and efficient radio communications mean that the capital is less remote, both conceptually and geographically, than it was 10 years ago. Every village now has its own primary school, and 2,500 health centres scattered across the island have greatly increased the chances of survival for children.

This last change, desirable as it is, has been an important factor in Java's spiralling population, which rose from 76 million in 1971 to 91 million in 1980, when 50 per cent of Javanese were under 17. Bali has seen a similar rapid increase. The government introduced a nationwide birth control campaign in 1970, which managed to reduce Indonesia's population growth rate from 2.7 per cent in 1970 to 2.1 per

As dawn breaks, pilgrims make their way along a mountain ridge towards the volcanic cone of Java's Mount Bromo, to pay annual homage to the fire-god they believe inhabits its crater. Indonesia is studded with more than 400 volcanoes, of which some 70 are active and a threat to the population.

cent in 1985. Despite the deceleration, widely regarded as one of the Third World's greatest family planning successes, this represents an increase of nearly 1.5 million people a year.

As the population of Java and Bali has grown, the peasants have pushed higher up the volcanic slopes, abandoning wet-rice farming for dry-rice cultivation. In the process, they have felled large areas of forest for farmland and fuel, exposing soil to erosion.

Even with the new fields that have been hacked out of the forests, only about a quarter of the population of these two islands own a substantial plot of land, and an army of landless labourers seeks work where it can. The government's answer to the problem is to resettle villagers from Java and Bali on the sparsely populated islands of Sumatra, Kalimantan, Sulawesi and Irian Jaya. In the course of the 1979–84 five-year plan, the government relocated 500,000 families—over two million people. Offering the prospect of a free plot, house and tools as an alternative to destitution, the scheme had more applicants than it could manage. But many of the relocated villagers found themselves in difficulties in their new surroundings, which were generally far less fertile than the soils they were accustomed to tilling. Even the authorities admit that finding worthwhile virgin sites will become increasingly difficult. Relocation also runs into opposition among the host islanders, who in places find themselves outnumbered by the newcomers.

Although much of the enormous island of Sumatra consists either of mangrove swamp or of rolling hills with poor soil, a rich alluvial plain in the north-east provides a prime area for cultivation.

Sumatra is not burdened with a vast population, and since the 19th century plantations on this plain have produced export crops—chiefly tobacco, rubber and oil palms. The island is also blessed with mineral wealth. From the last century onwards, it has been an important source of tin and now most of Indonesia's oil and gas are found off its shores. Thanks to all its resources, Sumatra is Indonesia's economic mainstay, pulling in about 70 per cent of the nation's external receipts.

To many of the ethnic groups scattered among the island's mountains and coastal reaches, such a statistic means little. They practise subsistence farming and may see little of the outside world. Sumatra's peoples include some of the most devoutly Muslim populations in Indonesia, and one race which is famous for its determined resistence to Dutch hegemony. The Acehnese of the island's northernmost tip formed an Islamic stronghold that fought the Dutch right up to the 20th century; today, they have been granted some autonomy in recognition of their independent spirit.

Kalimantan, 500 kilometres east of Sumatra, is Indonesia's largest territory and one of the world's most extensive tracts of primeval rainforest. Its steaming jungle houses a profusion of wildlife and exotic vegetation—orangutans and slow loris, flying lizards and hornbills, spectacular fungi and the garish, evil-smelling rafflesia, a parasitic plant that can produce a flower measuring a metre across and weighing nearly 10 kilograms. Human settlement is concentrated on the banks of the island's long, wide rivers. While the tangled hinterland is sparsely populated with tribal peoples practising slash-and-burn agriculture, oil

2

A house built by the Minangkabau of western Sumatra bears the rich decoration and curved gables typical of their architecture. Such dwellings accommodate extended families: men move into their wives' homes, which are repeatedly enlarged by extending the walls and adding a new roof.

production and logging have given rise to some busy cities near the coast.

The orchid-shaped island of Sulawesi, formerly known as the Celebes, lies east of Kalimantan and due south of the Philippines, whence Spanish Catholic missionaries set out in the 16th century to convert the natives of the north coast. Reconverted by Dutch Calvinists in the 19th century, the people of this area are among the most Christianized in Indonesia. But Sulawesi's spindly form and steep mountain ranges have cut other inhabitants off from change. Many of the isolated Toraja of the mountain fastnesses have never encountered Islam, let alone Christianity. Their culture is famous for devotion to the dead, which culminates in elaborate funerary feasts.

Another of Sulawesi's ethnic groups, the Bugis of the southern coast, is one of the world's most vigorous maritime peoples. Their distinctive gaff-rigged, black or green-sailed schooners still ply the old sea routes between Sulawesi, Kalimantan and Java, as they have for centuries past. From 8,000 to 10,000 vessels, each up to 300 tonnes deadweight, operate in Indonesian waters—perhaps the largest commercial sailing fleet left in the world. The Bugis' capital Makassar—now Ujung Pandang—was a centre for spice smuggling in the 17th century, before the Dutch monopolized the trade.

The spices were actually grown in the Moluccas, a group of islands east of Sulawesi. These remote volcanic specks still produce cloves, nutmegs and mace; they also have some of the richest fishing grounds in the world. The population is immensely varied. Halmahera, the largest island in the group but at 16,000 square kilometres smaller than Wales, is home to more

than 30 tribes speaking almost as many languages. Some of the islanders are Muslims or Christians; others still worship the nature spirits that their distant ancestors revered.

To the south of Sulawesi and the Moluccas, a chain of small, mountainous islands runs east from Java and Bali. Frequent droughts and the scarcity of level land to cultivate make this archipelago, collectively known as the Lesser Sundas, one of the poorest islands in Indonesia. The wildlife, however, is rich and bizarre. It includes the Komodo dragon, the world's largest lizard. Reaching three metres in length and weighing up to 150 kilograms, the "dragons" are swift and powerful enough to prey on wild pigs and deer.

Irian Jaya, the easternmost outpost of Indonesia, is a world unto itself. Its flora and fauna are akin to those of Australia rather than the rest of Asia.

Larger than California, it has a population of just over a million. Protected from the outside world by coastal mangrove swamps and jagged mountains, many of its Melanesian peoples remained stone-age hunter-gatherers almost to the present day. They are divided from one another not only by the terrain but also by ancient traditions of warfare, cannibalism and headhunting; often a tribe consisting of only a few villages speaks a language unintelligible to anyone else. Although building roads through the formidable mountains is out of the question in the foreseeable future, the people of Irian Jaya are increasingly encountering civilization in the shape of schools and medical centres supplied by air.

Irian Jaya's Melanesian peoples are the descendants of the first inhabitants of Indonesia, who arrived some 30,000

A statue of the Buddha sits meditating on a terrace atop the 1,200-year-old Buddhist temple of Borobudur in central Java. The world's largest Buddhist shrine, Borobudur was for centuries buried under volcanic ash until it was discovered by an English army colonel in 1814.

years ago. For millennia, they had the archipelago to themselves, but were eventually joined by mainland Malays who emigrated in two great waves, the first around 3000 B.C., the second about 300 B.C. By the second century B.C., many Indonesians were living in permanent communities, practising wet-rice agriculture, praying to nature gods and trading extensively with overseas lands.

A little later, Indonesia began to respond to an influence that would remain powerful for 1,500 years: that of the Indian subcontinent. Successive Indonesian kingdoms employed Brahmin scholars from India and adopted such imports as Buddhism and Hinduism, the Indian script and many Sanskrit loan words, together with Indian art and technology. Although Buddhism and Hinduism eventually retreated before Islam, cultural mementos of the period still linger. Bali remains obdurately Hindu, and elsewhere in Indonesia, self-professed Muslims—whose religion takes idolatry as anathema—regularly decorate old Hindu and Buddhist shrines with flowers or similar tokens. And the national emblem of this overwhelmingly Muslim country is the mythical bird called Garuda, the mount of the Hindu god Vishnu.

The earliest great Indianized state in Indonesia was Srivijaya, a Buddhist maritime power established in southern Sumatra. From the seventh to the 12th centuries, Srivijaya controlled the lucrative trade through the Malacca Straits. During that period, a succession of kingdoms sprang up in the fertile rice-growing area of central Java and competed to raise ever more splendid and burdensome monuments. The Sailendra dynasty erected the vast Buddhist temple of Borobudur in the eighth century; a few decades later another line, called Mataram, built the equally splendid Hindu temple complex of Prambanan to celebrate a victory over the Sailendras.

In the 10th century, for reasons now obscured by time, the focus of power in Java shifted to the east. And it was in eastern Java that Majapahit, the greatest of the early empires, was founded in 1292. It remained a major force for more than a century.

Majapahit could not be described as either Buddhist or as a strictly Hindu state, so thoroughly by then had the two religions become fused with each other and with local beliefs, including worship of nature spirits. Majapahit held sway over all Java and Bali; following the collapse of the Srivijaya empire, part of Sumatra became a dependency. According to a history by the court poet Prapanca, the kingdom also received tribute from vassals as far afield as Borneo, Sulawesi and the Moluccas. Prapanca's accuracy in matters that touched the honour of his ruler is questionable—he describes a royal dinner at which the king sang "lovable as the call of the peacock sitting in a tree, sweet as a mixture of honey and sugar, touching as the scraping noise of the reeds"—but the empire of Majapahit has nevertheless offered inspiration for 20th-century nationalist leaders scanning the past for some evidence of Indonesian unity.

Over the centuries, the leisured courtiers of Java's kingdoms developed a philosophy that stressed the need for self-control as the route to spiritual enlightenment. Orderly relationships with others would, they believed, lead to the desired state of inner calm. Etiquette and the art of conversation

41

A CHRONOLOGY OF KEY EVENTS

c. 3000 B.C. Proto-Malays from the Asian mainland begin migrating to Indonesia, eventually pushing the indigenous Australoid peoples into isolated pockets.

c. 100 A.D. Sophisticated kingdoms trading with other parts of Asia are established in Java and Sumatra.

c. 600–1100 The Buddhist kingdom of Srivijaya in southern Sumatra controls trade through the Malacca and Sunda Straits.

760–820 The Sailendra dynasty builds the great Buddhist monument of Borobudur in central Java.

c. 1250 Arab merchants begin introducing Islam to coastal kingdoms. Over the next few centuries the religion spreads throughout Indonesia.

1292–1453 An empire centred at Majapahit in eastern Java exercises a loose sovereignty over much of Indonesia. Its rulers and people worship the gods and goddesses of the Hindu pantheon (*below*).

1512 The Portuguese reach the Moluccas—the Spice Islands of east Indonesia.

1596 Dutch ships reach west Java.

1602 The Dutch East India Company is formed to exploit the eastern spice trade.

1619 The Company establishes a base (*above*) at Jakarta, which it renames Batavia. Through conquest and cessions from local rulers, the Dutch come to control most of Java by the end of the 17th century.

1799 The Dutch East India Company is bankrupted by its corrupt practices and reckless financial management. The Dutch government takes over Company possessions.

1811–1816 During the Napoleonic Wars, the British capture and govern the Dutch East Indies. In 1816, the Dutch regain control by treaty.

1825–1830 A rebellion known as the Java War threatens Dutch authority. Its leader, Prince Diponegoro, is exiled to Sulawesi.

1830 The Dutch introduce forced cultivation: peasants must devote a portion of their land to growing export crops for the government.

1870 Permission for Europeans to lease land opens an era of large plantations, especially in Sumatra.

1870–1910 The Dutch impose their rule on the outer islands of Indonesia.

Meanwhile, a war against the Aceh sultanate of northern Sumatra ends in Dutch victory. Their control of Indonesia is now complete.

1892 Oil starts to flow from wells in Sumatra. By the 1930s oil is Indonesia's second biggest export, after rubber.

1912 Merchants in Java found the Islamic Association, which develops into a nationalist movement protesting Dutch rule.

1927 The Indonesian Nationalist Party is formed under the chairmanship of Sukarno.

1942 The Dutch East Indies fall to the Japanese.

1945 On the Japanese surrender, Sukarno unilaterally proclaims the independence of the Indonesian republic.

1949 After attempting to reassert control by armed force, the Dutch accept United Nations mediation and pass sovereignty to Indonesia.

1963 Western New Guinea, now known as Irian Jaya, becomes part of Indonesia after the withdrawal of the Dutch.

1965 An attempted coup by junior army officers is blamed on a Communist plot. Government troops and mobs slaughter about 500,000 suspected Communists, including many Chinese. The army seizes power but retains President Sukarno as a figurehead.

1967 President Sukarno is replaced by General Suharto (*below*).

1975 Indonesia invades and subsequently annexes East Timor, a former Portuguese colony.

reached peaks of refinement, and the Javanese language developed its stratified complexity. The philosophy and its social ramifications reached down to every level of Javanese society. Admiring all that is complex and understated, the Javanese people acquired an aversion to anything coarse or obvious and came to avoid all displays of emotion. These Javanese values have now touched most Indonesians.

The arts that flowered in the early courts were informed by the philosophy of restraint. The intricate craft of batik cloth printing, using wax to keep dye from designated areas of the fabric, developed as an occupation for high-born ladies; it was considered a spiritual discipline. Live theatre and puppet plays enacted the stories of the Ramayana and the Mahabharata—Indian epics that pivot on the rivalries between semi-divine families—but the tales were given moral overtones of the conflict between refined and base feelings. These courtly diversions have long since gained the affection of every level of the population in Java and beyond. Batik is practically national dress, and puppet performances still draw villagers who assemble to enjoy the night-time coolness, smoke Java's distinctly clove-flavoured cigarettes and absorb yet again the ethical messages of the epics.

Marco Polo, the first European traveller to visit Indonesia, reached Sumatra on his way home from China in 1292. At that time, Java's Hindu-Buddhist culture was approaching its golden age, but new currents were already washing Sumatra. There, Marco Polo encountered many "idolaters", and noted disapprovingly of one mountain people that "each individual adores throughout the day the first thing that presents itself to his sight when he rises in the morning", but also discovered that many coastal inhabitants of Sumatra's northern tip were Muslims.

Islam was being brought to Indonesian shores by Arab and Gujarati traders, and was gradually extending its hold. By the end of the 16th century, most of Java embraced the new faith, as did seaboard peoples of the archipelago's other islands. Small sultanates established on the coasts gradually increased in power; by the early 15th century Majapahit was in a state of collapse, rent by internal conflicts and threatened from without.

Although Islam eventually spread to 90 per cent of Indonesians, those who encountered it reacted in very different ways. The Balinese—for reasons that remain mysterious—rejected it completely. The Javanese, steeped in their courtly traditions, accepted the forms of the religion, such as circumcision. But they retained their pre-Islamic philosophy almost intact. On the other hand, the Sundanese people of west Java became ardent Muslims, as did several Sumatran peoples.

Nowadays about half of Indonesia's Muslims are orthodox or *santri*; the other half—the *abangan*—are nominal believers, and lax often to the point of indifference in applying the laws governing prayer and diet. Indonesia's indigenous mystical nature worship is prominent among their beliefs, mixed with Hindu and Buddhist elements. Whereas the *santri* make a point of praying five times a day, learning Arabic and making at least one pilgrimage to Mecca, the *abangan* do little more than pray on formal occasions.

In 1512, when Islam was continuing to make inroads in Indonesia, another crucial ingredient was added to the cultural mix. Portuguese ships arrived in the archipelago's waters, auguring a European presence that became increasingly dominant over the next 400 years. The newcomers sought cloves and nutmegs—which at that time were found nowhere in the world but the Spice Islands—and fragrant sandalwood, which grew on the Lesser Sundas. Over the next few decades, the Portuguese established trading settlements in the Spice Islands, now the Moluccas, and on Flores and Timor.

The Portuguese soon encountered competition from the Dutch, who in 1602 founded their East India Company to spearhead the struggle for a monopoly of the immensely lucrative spice trade. In 1619, they succeeded in establishing Batavia, now Jakarta, in western Java, and from this permanent headquarters they expanded their influence, using a combination of force, judicious siding in local disputes and treaties with puppet leaders. By the end of the 17th century, they had become the uncontested sole cultivators and traders in the Spice Islands, though Portugal hung on in the eastern half of Timor until 1975.

Dutch colonial society quickly took on a distinct character of its own. The early officials of the East India Company married local women or lived with Asian concubines. The children of these unions were accepted into the European community, and after the first generation, Dutchmen preferred to marry women of mixed race rather than those of pure Indonesian blood. Men who had made a mixed marriage often sent their sons back to the Netherlands, but they themselves settled in Java permanently and kept their daughters there to marry the next

2

A young man marches his family's
ducks along a country road in Bali to
the flooded rice fields where they will
feed. He will stick his long pole into
the ground to serve as a beacon for the
birds which, after gorging on eels and
frogs, will gather round it in the
afternoon for the slow waddle home.

wave of emigrants. Dutchmen retained their wigs and heavy European dress, but many aspects of their new lifestyle contrasted with the bourgeois routine they had left. They spent freely, living in luxury in spacious villas, their wives attended by numerous slaves and diverted with local entertainments such as the shadow play.

For the first half of their long colonial tenure, the Dutch demanded little more than their hold on trade. Fortified bartering stations at river mouths usually marked the extent of their territorial control, and many parts of the archipelago, including much of Java's interior, remained oblivious of the Dutch presence.

Towards the end of the 16th century, a second Mataram dynasty had been founded in central Java in the lands of the early Hindu kingdom. The new power was Islamic but it retained the courtly style of the earlier Javanese kingdoms. In the early 17th century, Mataram conquered most of Java. Its subsequent turbulent history was dominated by wars with the Dutch and internal faction-fighting. In 1755 its territories were carved in two, and rival rulers established themselves in the neighbouring capitals of Jogjakarta and Solo. The Dutch East India Company, having spent far more than it could afford on military skirmishes, went bankrupt in 1799.

The Netherlands government at once took over the Company's East Indian possessions and the independence of Java's feudal princes was doomed. The Dutch stepped up their military presence. The first Governor General, Marshall Daendels, treated the princes as vassals and crushed rebellion with force. Meanwhile, Napoleonic France had incorporated the

Netherlands into its empire; in the course of the wars against Napoleon, the British invaded the Dutch East Indies in 1811. For the five years of British rule, Thomas Stamford Raffles, the British Lieutenant-Governor of Java who later founded Singapore, opposed feudalism and instituted many reforms to favour the peasantry.

In 1816 the archipelago was handed back to the Dutch. They continued the practice started by Daendels and Raffles of intervening at many junctures of native society. High taxes were imposed and discontent grew. Eventually it exploded into outright war. Between 1825 and 1830 a Javanese Muslim mystic, Prince Diponegoro, led a series of campaigns that cost about 200,000 Javanese and 8,000 European lives.

The capture and banishment to Sulawesi of Diponegoro, by this time a national hero, was of small comfort to the Dutch, who found themselves in dire economic straits. A solution was sought and found. In 1830 the colonial rulers imposed an infamous policy euphemistically called the Cultivation System, by which every village on Java was obliged to set aside part of its land—at first 20 per cent, later 33—to produce export crops such as coffee, sugar and indigo for sale at fixed prices to the government. With the world economy expanding at a terrific rate, the scheme was an unqualified financial success which essentially turned Java into one big Dutch plantation. The peasants, however, left without enough land to grow their own food, suffered deprivation and sometimes outright starvation.

Meanwhile, the Dutch were continuing to extend their control over the outer islands—a process that would be essentially completed by 1910. From

1870, forced cultivation in Java was largely abandoned and colonial attention swung to Sumatra, where empty land invited development. Entrepreneurs poured money into the island to develop profitable tobacco, rubber and sugar plantations. For a while, the Dutch East Indies were the biggest producers of sugar in the world. Towards the end of the century, tin mines and oilfields also came into operation. Chinese traders, small numbers of whom had been trickling into Indonesia for centuries, settled in much larger numbers at this time.

The Dutch population of the Indies increased from 22,000 in 1852 to 75,000 by 1900, the majority of them planters or entrepreneurs. Women came from the Netherlands in increasing numbers and, as the Dutch became a more self-contained group, the status of those of mixed race fell; they were eventually largely confined to menial jobs in the civil service, where all higher positions were occupied by Dutchmen. As contact with the mother country improved through the telegraph service and faster shipping, many Dutch families in Indonesia felt less constrained than before to cling to European habits unsuited to the climate: they adopted a modified version of Indonesian dress, took siestas and ate the local spicy dishes. The adoption of native habits disguised a growing gulf between rulers and ruled.

The Dutch in Indonesia spared little concern for the conditions of their subjects. They had no wish to spread education; thousands of Dutchmen in the Indies were available to fill all the demanding jobs. The abolition of forced cultivation had done little for the Javanese, who still had to pay heavy land taxes. Their population was rising rapidly and, with the best land already in cultivation, the peasants were finding it increasingly difficult to grow enough food to survive.

It was the public in the Netherlands rather than the colonialists who, upon hearing reports of appalling conditions among the Indonesians, demanded improvements. The Dutch government responded by investing in agricultural development and transport, in public health and education. By the early 1930s, a million pupils were attending schools. Technical, law and medical colleges were founded, and a few talented Indonesians even went to the Netherlands for higher education.

Opportunities for the growing corps of educated Indonesians to shape their country or even their own destinies were limited, however. The Dutch still occupied all administrative posts; Chinese immigrants dominated trade, and industry was practically nonexistent. Educated Indonesians soon focused their energies on nationalism.

One of the early channels for radical ideas was the Islamic Association. Founded in 1912 as an attempt to find a political role for Islam, it attracted a mass membership of both *santri* and *abangan* Indonesians. It was succeeded as a nationalist force by the Communist Party, which fomented revolution in the 1920s. It was not until 1927 that the party which was to play a major role in achieving independence was born. The Indonesian Nationalist Party was founded by a group of graduates led by a 26-year-old engineer named Sukarno (like many Indonesians, he used only one name). This was the man who would proclaim Indonesia's independence in 1945.

Within his own family, Sukarno had experienced the union of the archipelago's peoples that he preached to his countrymen. His father was nominally a Muslim Javanese, his mother was a Hindu from Bali—a very uncommon match for the period. Sukarno's father was a schoolteacher who instilled in his son the value of a Western education and somehow scraped together the money to send him to secondary school and to technical college in Bandung. But the boy was also steeped in Java's mystical culture, and to the end of his life his universe was that of the shadow plays, where endless struggle and conflict achieves a fleeting harmony.

As a schoolboy, Sukarno lodged with Umar Said Tjokroaminoto, the chairman of the Islamic Association, where he imbibed nationalist ideals. As he became politically active, the somewhat shy, withdrawn young man

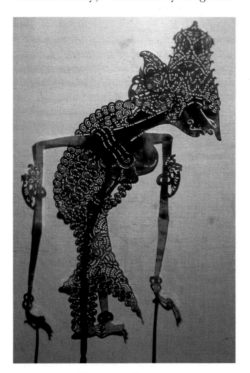

The delicate silhouette of a two-dimensional parchment puppet falls on a screen during a 10-hour performance of a tale from the Hindu Ramayana epic. Often staged with an orchestra, Javanese shadow-puppet theatre is one of the most popular performing arts in Indonesia.

found that he had a gift for oratory. When he graduated as an engineer, he resolved to devote his life to political activism—partly, no doubt, to give vent to the powers he had found within himself, partly because of a genuine concern for his countrymen's plight.

Sukarno made public appearances throughout Java on behalf of the Indonesian Nationalist Party, and he wrote many newspaper articles which preached passive resistance and noncooperation with the Dutch. In 1929 the colonial authorities responded by outlawing the movement and imprisoning Sukarno. On his release, two years later, he resumed his activities, spreading the idea of the Indonesian nation and the use of the Indonesian language. In 1933 he was banished to Flores in the Lesser Sundas; he remained in internal exile for 10 years. Peace was restored and the Dutch planters sipping beer on their verandas took comfort from the statement made by their Governor General de Jonge as the dissidents departed: "We have been here for 350 years with stick and sword and will remain here for another 350 years with stick and sword."

But during World War II another power, armed with a bigger stick and a sharper sword, arrived to shatter the dreams. Early in 1942, the Japanese conquered the Dutch East Indies in a matter of weeks. The rout of their colonial masters had a tremendous psychological effect on the Indonesians. Three years of Japanese occupation honed their aspirations further. In a bid to mobilize Indonesia in the war effort, the Japanese trained an Indonesian militia which later became the backbone of the Indonesian army. The Japanese also co-opted nationalist leaders such as Sukarno. While pur-

portedly expanding the Japanese cause the nationalists built up a popular following. With the disappearance of the Dutch into concentration camps, the Indonesians for the first time attained high government office, and Indonesian became the official language.

Although Japanese rule seemed more accommodating than that of the Dutch, disillusionment set in when the occupiers resorted to forced labour and food requisitioning. By late 1944, when it was clear that the Japanese were losing the war, the only way they could muster faltering Indonesian support was to promise independence. It was with the connivance of the Japanese commander that Sukarno made his Independence proclamation, two days after Japan surrendered to the Allies and six weeks before Allied forces, spearheaded by the British, landed to take control of the archipelago.

Soon the Dutch were back. Towards the end of 1945, civilians returned to the major cities of Java and Sumatra, and to many outlying islands. In early 1946, Dutch forces relieved the Allies.

But Dutch supremacy was not so easily restored. In the months after Sukarno's declaration, the euphoria of revolution swept the country. Old scores were settled and in some places traditional aristocratic élites were overthrown. Artists and writers produced a spate of powerful works evoking the spirit of the time. Enthusiasm for the new republic was, however, much stronger in Java and Sumatra than elsewhere; in 1946 the Dutch were able to set up an administration in Sulawesi which extended to many outer islands.

The Dutch then began to negotiate with the republican leaders over the possibility of creating a federal system which would leave the Netherlands in control of large parts of their former possession. The two parties achieved a broad agreement but reached stalemate over details. In 1947 the Dutch attacked the republican areas of Java and Sumatra in what was described as a "police action". They made some inroads and left the republicans torn by factional rivalries.

Further bloodshed was to follow. In September 1948, the Communist Party tried to commandeer the Independence war and transform it into a vehicle for general social revolution by attacking republican forces. It took two months of bitter fighting before Sukarno and his colleagues could stamp out the rebellion. That threat was hardly over when the Dutch mounted a second "police action". The Indonesians resisted fiercely.

As the guerrilla war continued, world opinion swung against the colonial power. Under pressure from the Americans, who were threatening to withdraw reconstruction aid to wartorn Holland, the Dutch finally agreed to transfer sovereignty. When they did so in 1949, it was in exchange for guarantees safeguarding Dutch investments in Indonesia. Partly for sentimental reasons, the Dutch insisted also on retaining one large possession—western New Guinea.

By the time the Dutch bowed out, Indonesia's leaders had agreed that their nation was to be a secular state. Sukarno had resisted all suggestions of creating an Islamic republic, which would have alienated the millions of Christians and other minorities, and threatened the country's unity. Indonesia was first set up as a federal system, but the idea of federation had been discredited in many Indonesians' eyes by its association with the departing

47

2

colonial power; in 1950 a new Constitution established a unitary state.

Sukarno was Indonesia's first president and he remained in power for 20 years. Together with his colleagues he had to create Indonesia's governing institutions from nothing, since the Dutch, resistant until the last to pleas for Independence, had not instituted even a minor degree of self-rule.

Until the late 1950s Indonesia experimented with a parliamentary system. A provisional assembly was set up in 1950 and the numerous political parties formed during the Independence struggle were granted seats in accordance with their presumed strengths. None had a majority, and quarrelsome, short-lived coalitions became the norm. The Nationalist Party which Sukarno had helped found was one of the largest. There were also religious parties, regional parties and the Communist Party—the PKI—which, recovering rapidly from the odium of the 1948 rebellion, was increasing its membership like wildfire in the countryside. It gained its popularity largely by undertaking welfare projects such as building schools, and in doing so became progressively less radical. It was not, however, offered a place in any of the coalitions. Sukarno allowed the other parties free play but he, as the only constant factor in government, wielded the ultimate power. And he had no compunction in overturning ministerial decisions when it suited his purpose to do so.

In 1955, elections were finally held. The number of parties in parliament increased as a result, instead of shrinking as most observers had hoped, and the coalition that resulted was ineffectual. A number of army officers, disappointed at the impasse, seized power in Sumatra and some of the other outer islands in 1957. Sukarno imposed martial law to contain the rebellion and loyal troops reoccupied Sumatra. Martial law gave the military a hold on power which it never relinquished.

Emboldened by his handling of the 1957 crisis, Sukarno became increasingly disenchanted with parliament: the concept of an opposition, he felt, was alien to South-East Asian traditions of consensus. In 1959 he moved to create what he called "Guided Democracy". Parliament was abolished. Under a changed Constitution which gave greater powers to the president, Sukarno created a non-party cabinet which included army chiefs.

Sukarno rallied immense loyalty as the father of Indonesian Independence and his genius for oratory carried the masses along. The nation accepted his increased powers with equanimity and even enthusiasm. But his move was to bring him new dangers. Previously he had manipulated events behind the scenes without accruing blame; now that he had openly taken a greater share of power, he would suffer in popular esteem from his mistakes.

Although increasingly authoritarian, Sukarno was no dictator: he had to rely on his skill as a manipulator to exert his will against the opposition of other powerful interests—the army, the parties, the regions and Islam. His charisma and political dexterity were his greatest assets. Because of his popularity, other powerful groups leaned on him for strength and he became skilled at playing one force off against another. The army valued their links with him and he kept his importunate military allies in check by threatening to bring the Communists into government. The PKI, with its grassroots organization, represented a colossal potential power: by the early 1960s it was the third largest Communist Party in the world in terms of membership, and the largest not in power. Sukarno gave his flirtation with the PKI extra plausibility by establishing cordial relations with Mao's China.

Political surefootedness, however, was no help to Sukarno in handling his most serious problem, the state of the economy. During World War II and the post-war struggle for independence, plantations and mines had been neglected; exports had plummeted. Peasant farms had suffered too, as a result of the widespread chaos and failure to maintain irrigation systems. Indonesia had been self-sufficient in rice in 1941, but for many years after the war it could not produce enough to feed its ever-growing population.

The President failed to tackle the crisis effectively. He talked of instituting land reforms but did little of substance to help the peasants. Large-scale agriculture and mining badly needed injections of foreign capital, but Sukarno was stridently hostile to the West and especially to anything that smacked of neo-imperialism. A mass of petty legislation and high taxes discouraged foreign investors. In 1957 Sukarno expelled virtually all of the Dutch nationals in the country and seized numerous foreign estates. Many of the remaining European and American businesses then pulled out of Indonesia, fearing the same fate.

This loss of foreign management skills dealt a serious blow throughout the Indonesian economy. The army took over the running of most of the newly nationalized industries and these were soon rife with corruption.

A MOUNTAIN SANCTUARY FOR THE DEAD

Hidden in the mountains of central Sulawesi, the Toraja people lived undisturbed by outsiders until the arrival of the Dutch in 1905. In their isolation they developed a unique set of beliefs and customs, most of which centred round death. Today, though some Toraja have converted to Islam or Christianity, many have clung to their ancient funerary rites and reverence for their ancestors.

Funerals literally cost fortunes. To send the deceased off into the next world, families may spend all they own on a riotous month-long banquet. To aid the ascent to heaven, the dead are entombed high in a sheer cliff, in holes accessible only by ladders. Lifelike effigies are placed in nearby niches.

Square wooden doors in a limestone burial cliff *(above)* **mark the resting places of Toraja corpses. Ranked effigies of the deceased** *(top)*, **also set into the cliff face, remind the living of the immanence of their ancestors' souls. Out of reverence, the effigies' clothes are regularly changed.**

2

Inflation rose to around 100 per cent per annum between 1961 and 1964.

The President resorted to morale-boosting gestures to prove Indonesia's greatness. In 1955, Indonesia had been the host to representatives of 29 African and Asian nations who met at Bandung in Java—a gathering that would result a few years later in the founding of the Non-Aligned Movement. From the time of the Bandung meeting, Sukarno saw it as his vocation to turn Indonesia into a world power. Especially in his latter years, he travelled the globe in style with a vast entourage. At home, colossal sums were expended on grandiose sports stadiums and monumental statues.

Sukarno also embarked on military adventures. Indonesia had for years been demanding without success that the Dutch hand over their one remaining possession in the area, western New Guinea. In 1961 matters were brought to a head when Indonesia sent in troops. The Americans, anxious to prevent the oil-rich nation from cutting any more links with the West, put pressure on the Dutch to acquiesce in the invasion. In 1963 they handed over the territory, though not without misgivings, since its small population had few ethnic, cultural or historical links with distant Jakarta.

The United Nations attempted to win safeguards for the new Indonesians, specifying that the people of the territory, now renamed Irian Jaya, should have a say in their own future. An "Act of Free Choice" was accordingly organized by Jakarta, though not until 1969. Instead of the universal plebiscite envisaged by the United Nations, only 1,022 Irian leaders were consulted. The government succeeded in eliciting the consent of each and

every one of them to membership of the nation into which their people had been forcibly incorporated six years earlier. But the continuing armed resistance to Indonesian rule shows that many Irianese are still not reconciled to government from Jakarta.

Sukarno's next diversionary tactic, a confrontation with Malaysia in 1963, was a failure that helped precipitate his own downfall. Violently opposed to British plans to create a federation between newly independent Malaya and the Borneo territories of Sarawak and Sabah, Sukarno tried to smash this "neo-colonialist conspiracy", first by roughhouse diplomacy, then by sending troops to invade Malaysian Borneo and even to parachute into mainland Malaya. But by 1965, with the army only half-heartedly participating, the campaign reached a stalemate.

While the gloss was wearing off Sukarno's foreign policy, matters were careering out of control on the domestic front. With exports at a virtual standstill, inflation raging at 500 per cent and the price of rice increasing ninefold, the nation was suffering from the effects of Sukarno's reckless economic policies. The Communist Party continued to attract supporters; Sukarno had kidney disease and was thought to be near death. Many became convinced that the Communists would shortly insinuate themselves into power. By 1965 a wide cross-section of Indonesians were unhappy with Sukarno's regime. They included not only members of the armed forces and the business community, but also students and devout Muslims and Christians, all of whom feared an imminent Communist takeover.

Although a coup was expected, the powers in Indonesia found themselves

At a market in the central Balinese
village of Ubud, traders sheltering
under bamboo sunshades display their
produce in ample wickerwork baskets.
The choice of fruit and vegetables on
sale includes bananas, chillies,
coconuts, mangoes and sweet potatoes.

51

2

unprepared when a leftist faction within the army and air force attempted to seize control on September 30, 1965. The conspirators captured and killed six out of seven generals whom they alleged were plotting an army insurrection against the President. Missing from the list of victims, however, was General Suharto, commander of the Strategic Reserve, a powerful back-up force whose support was essential if the coup was to succeed.

While President Sukarno vacillated, Suharto took firm steps to foil the attempted coup. He marshalled loyal forces and compelled the rebels to flee to central Java, leaving Jakarta in his hands. Having seized the initiative, Suharto showed no inclination to step out of the limelight.

To what extent the PKI was behind the coup has never been satisfactorily established. Tentative support from Jakarta's leading Communist newspaper on October 2 apparently pointed to at least some involvement, but it seems unlikely that the regional leadership—let alone the rank and file—knew anything of the plot.

Whatever the case, the entire PKI membership was to pay a terrible price. The country slowly succumbed to an orgy of violence, with PKI supporters the main targets, as the army set to eliminating its only real rival. South-East Asia had known no comparable episode of carnage since World War II. By the time the bloodbath ended in 1966, an estimated half a million Indonesians had been killed, with perhaps twice as many imprisoned. In 1977, Amnesty International estimated that as many as 100,000 political prisoners were still held in Indonesia, mainly in penal colonies on the outer islands. By 1980,

most of them had been finally released.

The onslaught was in part an attack by the army against the left. But it escalated into general unrest and chaos by touching deep religious and economic antagonisms among Indonesia's people. Sukarno's secular state had angered Indonesia's devout Muslims. Many of these were large landowners, so they also felt personally threatened by Sukarno's promises to carry out land reform. In contrast, most of those who had joined the Communist Party were *abangan*, nominal Muslims; politics had added an extra strain to tensions already existing between them and the *santri*.

While in some areas it was the army that carried out the massacres, in many parts local Muslim groups, albeit often with weapons supplied by the army, did the killing. The targets were not just known Communists, but also ethnic Chinese, who were suspected of links with mainland China and disliked as outsiders.

Sukarno could do nothing to halt the terror. After the attempted coup, he tried to act as though authority was still in his hands, but discovered that Suharto was now the effective leader of the country. Suharto did not bother to challenge Sukarno's official pronouncements; he merely paid no attention to them and issued his own edicts. Frequently, Sukarno was forced into embarrassing climbdowns.

The army was in no hurry to strip Sukarno of the trappings of power. They knew that he was still a hero to many Indonesians. While others approved Sukarno's shackling, Suharto was still an unknown quantity and the people needed time to learn to trust him. But after an unsuccessful attempt by Sukarno in February 1966 to assert

his authority in a controversial cabinet reshuffle, the army forced him formally to delegate supreme authority to General Suharto. For another year, Sukarno remained president. He spoke in public as if he was still the man who decided Indonesia's fate, but his views were ignored and his former policies overturned. In 1967, the provisional military government finally felt strong enough to relieve him of his office and name Suharto acting president. Sukarno died in 1970, but his regime—known today in Indonesia as the "Old Order"—had already passed away with the attempted coup of 1965.

Pragmatic, cautious and private, Suharto was the antithesis of his volatile and populist predecessor. The son of a landless peasant, he was born in 1921 in central Java, and spent his boyhood within a day's journey of the courts of Jogjakarta and Solo. He entered the Dutch East Indian army at the age of 18 and rose rapidly in its ranks. During the 1945–49 war against the Dutch he led guerrilla troops; after the transfer of sovereignty he remained a professional soldier, reaching the rank of major-general by 1962. He was universally admired as a brave and astute soldier, but until the 1965 attempted coup he appeared to have little interest in government. He soon revealed himself, however, as a brilliant politician whose judgement and timing could rarely be faulted.

While Sukarno's overriding aim had been to foster the idea of the Indonesian nation and its greatness, Suharto was able to take nationhood and unity as a given and concentrate on more concrete matters. Hence many of the policies of Suharto's "New Order" took Indonesia in radical departures

Schooners, built and sailed by the Bugis people of Sulawesi, lie moored by a quayside in Jakarta after bringing sawn timber from Borneo. The Bugis are renowned seafarers who still ply the extensive trader networks between Indonesia's many islands.

from Sukarno's line. In the foreign field, Suharto retained affectionate links with the Non-Aligned Movement—but he severed the bonds that Sukarno had forged with China and turned instead towards the non-Communist countries, particularly the United States and Japan, for economic aid. Suharto even buried the hatchet with Malaysia, formally establishing links with Indonesia's former enemy in 1967, the year ASEAN was created.

Only once in the first 20 years of his military administration did he embroil Indonesia in a foreign adventure of the kind Sukarno undertook in Irian Jaya. Suharto's goal was the former Portuguese colony of East Timor. The colonial forces had fled their possession in 1975 after one of East Timor's three main political parties seized power. But after a brief civil war it was another party, the leftist Revolutionary Front of Independent East Timor (Fretelin) which gained control. The spectre of a Cuba in Indonesia's midst proved too much for Suharto's anti-Communist temper. In December, Indonesian troops invaded East Timor, and in 1976 East Timor became a province of Indonesia. But Fretelin went into the rugged, bush-covered hills to wage guerrilla war. Ten years later the fighting was still going on, having claimed the lives of about 10 per cent of the island's 200,000 people.

Elsewhere in the country, though, the first 20 years of Suharto's New Order were relatively calm. To an extent, the stability was imposed by force rather than by consent. From the start, Suharto controlled the two institutions that matter in Indonesia—the army and the civil service. Freedoms have remained much narrower than they were even under Sukarno. But among the peasantry, opposition has in any case been muted by memories of the traumatic 1965 bloodbath, while both peasants and the influential middle class have benefited from the prosperity generated by the New Order.

Suharto reversed Sukarno's policy towards foreign investors who, after a period of scepticism, once more flocked in, attracted by Indonesia's range of natural resources, especially its low-sulphurcrude oil. The oil was discovered by chance in 1883, when a Dutch planter in north Sumatra noticed a torch burning in a native shed. When he asked what fuelled the flame, his host showed him a nearby spring covered with a thick, tarry skin. That chance discovery led to the formation of the Royal Dutch Shell Company, which still has residual interests in Indonesia. But today, oil production is under the overall control of Pertamina,

Flare stacks burn off excess gas at an oil drilling installation in the swampy delta of the Mahakam river in east Kalimantan. Indonesia produces 2 per cent of the world's oil, enough to satisfy 75 per cent of its domestic energy needs and bring in two thirds of its foreign-exchange earnings.

the State oil and gas company set up during the Sukarno era.

Indonesia's oil, which it can sell at a premium over most other grades, has been both boon and burden: the key to the country's economic progress, but also an easy corrupter and a spawner of grandiose visions. During the 1970s and early 1980s, it dominated all other resources, bringing in 70 per cent of total export receipts. Today, 70 per cent of Indonesia's oil comes from

Sumatra, 20 per cent from Kalimantan and 5 per cent from Irian Jaya. Production is falling as reserves shrink, but Pertamina has diversified into natural gas production. It is now the largest exporter of liquefied natural gas in the world; Japan and South Korea take most of its output.

The oil windfall and better economic management allowed Suharto to tackle many development problems that defeated Sukarno. Between 1972

and 1978, for example, over 25,000 primary schools were built and the number of doctors multiplied by five.

Oil money also poured into industrial projects. In the 1970s, Indonesia concentrated on developing labour-intensive industries such as plywood and batik cloth printing. Now the emphasis has shifted to engineering, electronics and oil-derived products such as fertilizer. The nation manufactures motorcycle and automatic parts under

Children congregate round the attendant at a rudimentary petrol station in southern Sumatra. The jerry cans arrayed at the front of the booth contain locally extracted crude oil, diesel, fuel for cookers and lamps, and petrol for the motorcycles owned by one in 30 Indonesians.

licence and makes aeroplanes in a joint venture with Spanish interests. As an exporter, overpopulated Indonesia, with its low rates of pay, has an edge over regional competitors such as Malaysia or even Thailand. But growing Western protectionism has hindered the country's aim of boosting its non-oil exports.

Agriculture, like manufacturing, benefited from the easy oil money. As recently as 1977, Indonesia had to import one third of the world's surplus rice to feed its population. In 1984, however, it became a rice exporter for the first time in more than 40 years. The turnaround came as a result of new irrigation schemes, the introduction of pest-resistant rice strains, larger storage capacity and increased credit for rice farmers. The attainment of self-sufficiency in a society that equates rice with prosperity has been a cause of great pride.

Even the long-neglected plantation sector attracted new attention in the early 1980s, when Indonesia began to concern itself seriously with its prospects when the oil ran dry. By the mid-1980s, the area under plantation—chiefly of sugar cane, rubber trees and oil palms—was growing at the rate of nearly one million hectares annually. Most of the new plantings were in Kalimantan and Sumatra.

The military have been deeply involved in every move to develop Indonesia's resources. Indeed, seeing itself both as a source of stability and a force that can propel the country to prosperity, the army lays claim to a permanent role in the direction of all civilian life. Its major role in business started with the seizure of Dutch assets under Sukarno. Since then, the lines between the armed forces, government and industry have become ever more blurred. In the first two decades of the New Order, hundreds of pensioned-off generals were granted nominal directorships on the boards of government corporations. After 1982, not only were Indonesia's president and vice president retired generals; so were a third of the cabinet, and a quarter of the seats in the *Dewen Perwakilan Rakyat*, the country's largely ceremonial (but occasionally awkward) parliament, were reserved for them too. At every level of government—provincial, district and sub-district—the armed forces' reach is evident; even village chiefs are often retired sergeants.

The other ubiquitous fact of Indonesian public life is corruption. It augments meagre civil servants' wages, speeds up business applications and helps traders avoid the full weight of their annual tax burden. At these petty levels, most Indonesians resignedly accept it as virtually the only force that keeps the ponderous bureaucracy going. But they resent the large-scale venality that has brought fortunes to those at the apex of Indonesian society. Some efforts have been made to clean up the system. The ports, for example, used to be so notorious for devious practices that in 1985 President Suharto took the bizarre step of pensioning off his entire customs service and putting a Swiss contractor on the docks to assess duties.

Complex and deeply compromising links exist between senior army personnel and merchants. Many of the latter are Chinese Indonesians, who still occupy the commanding heights of the economy. Most of the suspect business ties were cemented during the first days of Independence, when divisional army commanders—Suharto himself

Palm trees fringing a sandy shore in the south-east of Bali highlight the tropical beauty that has made the isle Indonesia's prime tourist destination. Most visitors are drawn to the coast, which offers superb beaches, surfing, and skin-diving over coral reefs.

among them—coped with inadequate funding from Jakarta by starting their own businesses in league with non-native Indonesians. Ostensibly the purpose was to supply and feed their troops, but often immense personal fortunes accrued along the way. Ever since, the Chinese have paid out huge quantities of protection money to their associates in the armed forces.

Indonesians who are unhappy with the way the army is running their country have few legitimate outlets for their complaints. The broadcasting networks are government-owned and controlled; the print media, fearful of any government interference, exercises severe self-censorship and addresses controversial subjects only by innuendo and analogy. Golkar, Indonesia's main political party under Suharto, is controlled by the military. Government pressure on the electorate has ensured a large majority for Golkar at every general election. The left was wiped out in the pogrom of 1965, and since 1966 the Communist Party has been outlawed.

In the opposition vacuum, the country's Muslim community has become the main channel of protest. A radical minority, deeply influenced by the worldwide Islamic political resurgence of the 1980s, have been critical of the administration's obsession with development and offended by a perceived indifference to Islam's strictures by senior members of the government.

The government, correctly viewing the Muslim right as its one remaining political threat, has endeavoured to eliminate ideology from politics. The official state philosophy, called Pancasila—five principles—is a programme calling for belief in God, humanitarianism, national unity based on con-

sensus and representation, and social justice. Conspicuously lacking from the list of objectives is any mention of a specific religion. In addition, the government has consistently made life difficult for religious zealots. In 1972 it forced four Islamic parties to merge together against their will as the United Development Party (PPP). The PPP leaders forged ties with government which gave them at least a hearing, but their effectiveness was steadily eroded by internal rifts and by government decrees that included forbidding the party to use as its symbol the holy Kaaba stone in Mecca.

Deprived of an influential voice in national politics, radical Islam began expressing itself in violence. An unruly mosque meeting in Jakarta in 1984 was followed by a spate of bomb and arson attacks on Chinese businessmen, a Catholic seminary and the Buddhist monument of Borobudur. The government acted fast and uncompromisingly; troops sent in to crush the riot in Jakarta fired on the crowd and killed at least 40 people.

Despite such rumblings of discontent, there is a feeling among most Indonesians that their country has come of age after two decades of frenetic nation-building under Sukarno and another two decades of more tangible achievement under Suharto. In this respect the country's 40th anniversary, celebrated with a month-long round of military parades and cultural events in 1985, had a special significance. In Java's complex culture, people measure their lives by cyclical five-year periods called *windus*, and a person with eight *windus* behind him is believed to have entered the mature and fulfilling period of life. As for a man or woman, so also for a nation.

ANCIENT TRADITIONS OF A JAVANESE COURT

The royal city of Jogjakarta in central Java is a survival from the island's monarchic past and is still its cultural hub. It was founded in 1755 after a power struggle within the ruling Mataram dynasty, which retained enormous respect and influence even while the Dutch were extending their own government over Java. Prominent in the 20th-century struggle against Dutch rule, the Sultan of Jogjakarta was made Governor of the city and surrounding province after Independence, retaining much of his ancestors' temporal authority.

Jogjakarta inherited and refined the elaborate artistic culture developed in earlier Javanese kingdoms. The dance, theatre, music, architecture and handicrafts patronized by the court drew on a rich fusion of native Indonesian, Buddhist and Hindu influences. But the rulers of Jogjakarta were Muslim, and its greatest displays were on Islamic feast days. Today, the Sultan's family still vigorously fosters Java's courtly arts, as well as celebrating the high points in the Muslim calendar with most of the pomp of former times.

Accompanied by courtiers, a son of Jogjakarta's Sultan officiates at a Muslim festival held in the palace. The gold umbrella is the prerogative of royalty; other colours used to be associated with different ranks in the Javanese social hierarchy.

Serpents and a giant's head adorn a rail round the palace ballroom. The images represent numbers—snakes, for example, are the guardians of the eight winds and thus mean eight. Together the carvings show the date the ballroom was built: 1853 in Javanese chronology, equivalent to 1923 A.D.

MAINTAINING THE STYLE OF A VENERABLE PALACE

**One of the Sultan's corps of cleaners
dusts the teak pillars and porcelain
pots that surround the Golden
Pavilion, the innermost reception and
ceremonial area of the palace.**

The palace at the heart of the city of Jogjakarta dates back to the 18th century; within its encircling walls stand quarters for the Sultan's extensive family, ornate state rooms and spacious open-sided pavilions. An army of retainers care for the buildings and their inmates.

Today's palace used to be the core of a more extensive complex which included a mosque, markets, parade grounds and royal pleasure gardens. These outer structures are no longer part of the palace proper, but many of the houses beyond the inner enclave are still owned and occupied by relatives of the Sultan.

Ladies-in-waiting to the Sultan's wives file through a courtyard to bring them tea.

A court attendant rests in the shade of a pavilion after completing his daily tasks; out of respect, he faces the Sultan's residence.

THE NOBLE ART OF DANCE

In Jogjakarta's heyday, dance was one of the arts most assiduously cultivated. The star roles were generally reserved for aristocrats, though members of the lower orders took supporting parts. Only in 1918 was the first classical dance school established beyond the palace walls for those who wanted to learn the discipline. Now Jogjakarta has about 20 dance organizations, and performances both in and outside the palace establish standards of accomplishment for the country.

Many of the dances dramatize stories from two Indian epics, the Ramayana and the Mahabharata.

While a chorus and soloists sing an accompaniment in nasal tones, the performers move through a series of positions, angular yet fluid, suggesting emotion with subtle hand gestures. Performances within the palace are choreographed strictly according to tradition, but some of the outside establishments experiment with new styles.

Dances are accompanied by the traditional Javanese gamelan orchestra of up to 30 instruments, mostly percussive. The drums, xylophones and many varieties of gong create a complex, shimmering texture of sound.

Flanked by the members of a gamelan orchestra, a uniformed performer plays upon brass gongs.

Two Javanese dancers enact in stylized movement an episode from the Ramayana in which the hero, Rama *(right)*, draws comfort from his younger brother, Lesmana. Both men wear one of the many traditional batiks of the Jogjakarta court draped over their patterned trousers. Their armbands, necklets, wings and headgear are made of leather and painted gold.

REVIVING PAST PAGEANTRY

On the Islamic feast day of Garebeg Besar, the citizens of Jogjakarta take part in lively celebrations that combine religion with the traditions of old court life. In a procession headed by the Sultan or one of his sons, huge offerings of rice, vegetables and sweetmeats are carried from the palace to the mosque in the city's main square. Here, the mountains of food are distributed among the crowds. Everyone tries to obtain a share of the offering to ensure well-being and to safeguard against bad luck.

In the past, the Sultan's parade was accompanied by 800 palace guards. The Sultan's retinue was disbanded during World War II, however, and today their place is taken by civilian volunteers.

Residents of Jogjakarta, wearing traditional batik sarongs and blue shirts, march through the streets in rehearsal for the Garebeg Besar procession. On the day of the festival the men will don the military costumes of the old palace guard.

The hilt of an Indonesian dagger juts from the belt of a marcher; his brass pouch bears the Sultan's crest.

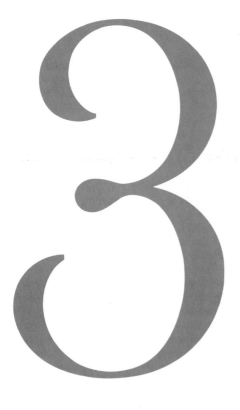

Silhouetted against Kuala Lumpur's city hall and a colonial clock tower, the domes and minarets of the Jame Mosque are a symbol of identity to Malaysia's largest native race. Allegiance to Islam is one feature that sets the politically dominant Malays apart from other ethnic groups.

A PARTNERSHIP
OF RACES

Between the two limbs of Malaysia's territory lie 700 kilometres of tropical sea, giving the country an oddly dislocated appearance on the map. On the ground, though, West Malaysia— the peninsula descending southwards from Thailand—bears a family resemblance to East Malaysia, which comprises the states of Sarawak and Sabah in northern Borneo. In both halves of the nation the land slopes up gently at first from mangrove swamps at the sea's edge, then rises abruptly to a mountainous spine. In both halves, too, jungle is abundant: despite extensive logging operations in recent years, rainforest still covers more than 70 per cent of the land— a higher proportion than in any other ASEAN country except for Brunei.

The rainforest of East Malaysia, however, is far more extensive than that of the west: indeed, the Malaysian and Indonesian sections of Borneo together make up the largest tract of untouched rainforest in the whole of South-East Asia. All the towns of any importance in Sarawak and Sabah are strung along the coast; neither roads nor railways slice a path through the forested interior.

In West Malaysia, unbroken rainforest is confined to the central mountain ridge. On lower ground, stretches of jungle are interspersed with villages surrounded by rice fields, with plantations of regimented rubber trees and oil palms, and with dynamic modern cities. The contrast between the primeval bush in the Pahang Hills and the glass towers of nearby Kuala Lumpur is as stark as any in Asia. Cobras occasionally slither into lush suburban gardens; elephants are now rare south of the Thai border, but tigers still roam parts of the countryside.

The wilderness encroaches because people are few: Malaysians number only 15 million. In Sabah and Sarawak, the density is very light indeed. But throughout Malaysia, the population makes up in complexity what it lacks in numbers.

The main indigenous inhabitants of peninsular Malaysia are the Malays: farmers and fishermen descended from migrants who arrived from mainland Asia around 300 B.C. In Sarawak and Sabah are found various tribal peoples, whose ancestors arrived in this part of the world from the Asian hinterland even earlier than the forebears of the Malays. The Iban, the most numerous ethnic group in Sarawak, cultivate rice by the slash-and-burn method and recall a warlike past as headhunters. The Kadazan, a more peaceable people, predominate in Sabah.

In addition to its various indigenous groups, Malaysia also accommodates Chinese and Indian populations so large as to make the Malays a minority in their native land, comprising just 47 per cent of the population. In combination with other native inhabitants such as the Iban and Kadazan—

3

A vendor of Chinese noodle soup pedals his stall to an outdoor pitch in Penang. Other mobile stalls serve Malay skewered chicken or Indian pancakes. Malaysians of all races are addicted to snacks, and they willingly sample the specialities of different culinary traditions.

known, like them, as *bumiputras*, "sons of the soil"—the Malays make up a small majority, 59 per cent. Chinese account for 32 per cent of the population and Indians for 8 per cent. Engendering both rich diversity and occasional bitter division, Malaysia's ethnic arithmetic informs all social, economic and political calculations in the country today.

The Chinese and Indians are to be found in cities throughout Malaysia, East and West, and some parts of the countryside as well. They are especially well represented along the densely populated western flank of the peninsula. Indeed, the ethnic mix in the small towns of these parts makes them microcosms of the nation.

One such community is Rantau, a little town near mainland Malaysia's western coast. On either side of the trunk road which briefly turns into Rantau's main street stand terraces of two-storey, open-fronted, tile-roofed dwellings. Upstairs in these "shophouses", the combined homes and workplaces of the Chinese, children sit from dawn to dusk watching Cantonese or Hokkien dialect videotapes—a steady diet of Hong Kong soap opera which will sustain them until they reach seven and go to school. On the ground floor, their fathers, dressed in white singlets and shorts, run general stores and restaurants and modest wholesale businesses. Outside in the street, Chinese chefs fry noodles at open-air stalls and take orders from truck drivers pausing for refreshment.

Just beyond the Chinese shophouses are the carved wooden stilt dwellings of the Malays. Outside them, sarong-clad peasants tend flowers and fruit trees in spacious gardens overlooking irrigated rice fields and sometimes a few rows of rubber trees. A group of Malay men gossip animatedly in the nearby coffee house; their wives gather to chat on the verandas in front of some of the houses. The mosque where the Malays congregate every Friday to worship stands on the outskirts of town; scattered among the homes are chapel-sized prayerhouses where the pious repair to pray five times a day.

The Malay smallholdings adjoin large company-run estates growing oil palm and rubber trees. Outside the town, past the police station, the fruit market and the bus depot, one comes eventually to the plantation headquarters and the cramped compounds of the Indians employed to tap the rubber trees and harvest the fruit of the oil palms. Lines of men and sari-clad women labour together in the dappled shade of the leaves. A brightly painted temple dedicated to the Hindu lord Subrahmanya is glimpsed between the rows of trees.

The division of occupations exemplified by Rantau goes back to imperial times, when the British—anxious not to disturb traditional local society—left the Malays down on the farm and encouraged rootless immigrants to develop modern sectors of the economy. But since Independence, strong economic growth coupled with positive discrimination for indigenous peoples have gone some way to dissolving the colonial-era rigidities. The world's largest producer of tin, rubber and palm oil, Malaysia has also become a manufacturer and major oil producer. *Bumiputras* are heading in increasing numbers for the cities in search of jobs at all levels in industry and government-funded university scholarships.

Nowhere are the new wealth and the new multiracial middle class more

Members of Malacca's Chinese community make offerings to their gods and ancestors in the city's Cheng Hoon Teng Temple. Although Islam is the state religion of Malaysia, the Constitution guarantees freedom of worship to its non-Malay citizens.

obvious than in Kuala Lumpur. The capital and its environs are home to over a million people—one in every 14 Malaysians. Yet a century ago it was just a collection of Chinese tin-miners' shacks sited at the highest navigable point of the silt-laden River Kelang; the city's name translates, unappetizingly, as "muddy estuary".

Some of Kuala Lumpur's wealthier suburbs are reminiscent of the colonial heyday earlier this century: villas set among orchids and hibiscus that provide oases of green and quiet. But much of the charm that once lured expatriates back to "KL" for second and third tours of duty has vanished in the last few years of hectic growth.

The mock-Moghul clocktower which dominates the main 19th-century administration building now seems a diminutive toy in comparison with the soaring headquarters of Malaysia's new corporations, many crowned with a helipad. Ministerial offices have been shifted from prefabricated, two-storey buildings to a hexagonal, 45-storey tower with a gleaming white-tiled exterior and a brown marble interior. An expensive reorganization of main boulevards begun in the 1970s was completed in the mid-1980s, just in time to be overwhelmed by the rise in traffic occasioned by the motormania afflicting every self-regarding aspirant to the middle class.

In the past, the different races occupied distinct areas of the city. But on the smart new estates that have sprung up on former rubber land the government has made a deliberate attempt to break the pattern. The salaried managers and the skilled workers of all races who have moved in have become accustomed to living cheek-by-jowl with their equivalents from other ethnic backgrounds. And the Selangor Club in the city centre, where generations of white planters sipped their gins, has become a congenial watering hole for the new political and business élite of every creed and colour.

Kuala Lumpur's new wealth is founded upon a centuries-old tradition of trade. Soon after settling on the peninsula around 300 B.C., the Malays began to exploit their position on the sea route between China and the West. By about 100 A.D., they had established trading links with India and China.

Absorbing cultural influences from India especially, communities on the peninsula coalesced over the centuries into small Hindu or Buddhist states. In the 15th century, one of these states

3

rose to pre-eminence in the region. Its name was Malacca, and it had the good fortune to be sited at the narrowest point on the Straits of Malacca, one of the world's most heavily travelled waterways, as well as to be ruled by a succession of strong princes. It became a great trading centre, renowned as an entrepôt for pepper, edible birds' nests, tortoise shells, camphor, pearls, gold and tin. Its court became a legend for wealth and opulence.

After a succession struggle in 1444, Muzaffar Shah, a zealous adherent to Islam, ascended the throne and made Malacca a Muslim state. He adopted the title of sultan, and his successors followed suit. Islamic elements were interpolated into the elaborate court

pageantry inherited from the Hindu-Buddhist period. Previously, Islam had touched only isolated spots on the peninsula, but thereafter conversion was rapid. Malacca's religious influence even spread via trade and matrimonial links to Borneo: the King of Brunei, who maintained loose control over the northern coast of the island, became a convert and began to style himself sultan.

During the height of its power, at the start of the 16th century, Malacca ruled much of the Malay Peninsula and part of Sumatra. But its golden age lasted little more than a century. Portugal seized the capital in 1511 and the sultan fled. But the Portuguese only wanted Malacca as a trading post;

they penetrated no farther into the country, and neither did the Dutch who took Malacca from Portugal in 1641. Meanwhile, the Malaccan aristocracy founded new dynasties elsewhere on the peninsula and re-created the pomp of the old court.

More than a century elapsed between the Dutch seizure of Malacca and the arrival of the colonial power that was to make the most impact on Malaysia. In 1786, the British took their first bite of the country, securing the island of Penang from a local sultan. In 1824, the Dutch ceded Malacca to Britain. From 1826, Penang, Malacca and Singapore were administered as a single unit, the "Straits Settlements". Encouraged by the order that

A VILLAGE UNDER ONE ROOF

The Iban, the most populous ethnic group in Sarawak, recall a turbulent past when every community was at war with its neighbours, and rival bands preserved the heads of their victims as ghoulish battle trophies. Faced with the constant threat of raids, as many as 70 families would live together in shared homes up to 260 metres long. Raised on stilts for extra protection, the houses were usually sited on the banks of rivers, which provided water, food and easy access by canoe.

Today peace reigns, and some Ibans now take jobs in the state's fast growing coastal oil towns. Most, though, still practise shifting cultivation in the forested interior, and choose to live in longhouses like their ancestors before them. Inside the bamboo-and-thatch structures, separate families occupy individual rooms articulated by a wide corridor running the length of the building—an arrangement that permits some privacy in a highly public lifestyle.

A longhouse flanks the river Rejang, its only link with the outside world.

British rule had brought, Chinese and Indian traders set up shop in Penang and Malacca. These early settlers, the Chinese especially, integrated themselves into local life. While retaining their own religious rites, they learnt to speak Malay and cook Malayan food.

Later generations of immigrants were not so easily assimilated. From the mid-19th century many Chinese, forced to leave their homeland by revolutions, floods and famines, came to exploit Malaysia's tin. The West had imported modest amounts of this metal for centuries but the industrial revolution, by stimulating demand for an inert coating that protected against corrosion, expanded the market hugely. Tin-plated canning for food became commonplace. The Malays lacked the capital and skills to intensify the mining operations; instead, sultans leased land to immigrants from China who organized gangs of their compatriots to dig up the metal.

The Malays thought of the newcomers as temporary residents, and the Chinese themselves concurred. They retained their own customs and stayed out of local politics. Coming from many different regions of southern China and speaking numerous dialects, they were obsessed by intrigues within their own community. The rivalries grew so bitter and intense that the years between 1855 and 1875 are remembered in Malaysia as the era of the "Wars of the Chinese Miners".

The strife had its origins in gambling quarrels, which led in turn to murders. Revenge killings sparked off battles between rival Chinese secret societies, driving thousands of Chinese in flight from one sultanate to another.

The disorder caused by the feuding eased the way for the imposition of British rule over the peninsula. In the early 1870s the anarchy was disrupting tin exports; Chinese and European middlemen in the Straits Settlements besought the British government to re-establish law and order. In 1874 the imperial power concluded a treaty with a pretender to the sultanate of Perak which marked a new phase in colonial history. In exchange for British recognition and support, the sultan

Men repair fishing nets and dogs snooze in the shared section of the longhouse. The door to one family's private area is on the right.

3

accepted a British "Resident" who in theory had no executive powers but in fact quickly established himself as the *de facto* ruler. In subsequent years three other sultanates in the middle of the Malay Peninsula were similarly co-opted into the British Empire.

In 1896 a federal government was established at Kuala Lumpur for the Federated Malay States, as the four sultanates had become known. The sultans still retained the trappings of power, but the reality had been discreetly removed. There remained five sultanates on the Malay Peninsula that resisted being incorporated into the federation. All of them, however, came under considerable British control at the end of the 19th century.

Well before any of the mainland sultanates had acquiesced to the British ascendance, part of the Sultan of Brunei's territory passed into British hands as a result of the escapades of an extraordinary English adventurer. James Brooke, the son of a wealthy employee of the East India Company, was born in India and remained under the spell of the East throughout his life. To the age of 35 he served as a military officer in India, but then, craving some more glorious destiny, he set sail in his own ship for Sarawak. He found the province in a state of anarchy, its various tribes at war with each other and piracy rife along the coast. Brooke used his schooner to control the piracy and his charisma to win over the various native factions. Soon he had established his authority as the only man capable of keeping control in the area. In recognition of his services, Brooke was formally installed by the Sultan's uncle, the governor of Sarawak, as its ruler in 1841. He remained rajah until his death in 1868, when his nephew—

Three variations on the traditional stilt-house manifest the pleasure that Malays take in immaculate homes and well-tended gardens. These quite spacious structures belong to the better-off; most people live in smaller, one-storey dwellings.

later followed by his great-nephew—succeeded to the throne of the "White Rajahs". The unlikely dynasty endured for a century.

In the meantime, North Borneo—the area today known as Sabah—had also entered the British sphere of influence. It was leased from the Sultan of Brunei by an enterprise called the British North Borneo Company, which in 1881 was granted a Royal Charter. The company made a modest profit by cultivating tobacco and by exporting birds' nests for Chinese soups. It was supposed to administer and develop the territory internally while leaving its foreign relations to the British government. In practice neither the company nor the government interfered much in the affairs of this under-populated backwater, though British missionaries did spread Christianity among the area's tribal peoples.

The Malay Peninsula, in contrast, was profoundly affected by the British, for it was their endeavours that encouraged the bulk of the immigration which has deeply divided the country until this day. British entrepreneurs modernized tin extraction, replacing labour-intensive pit mines with alluvial dredges that turned great tracts of the peninsula into moonscapes. The British also provided the infrastructure to shift the metal, cutting roads and railways through the mountains and throwing bridges across fast-flowing rivers. The tin industry multiplied in size and, in response to the demand for miners, the Chinese population—roughly 150,000 in 1874—grew to over two million by 1911.

The Chinese were not destined to remain mere tin miners for long. Endowed with colossal enterprise and drive, many of them were busy carving themselves a firm niche in property, manufacturing and money-lending by the beginning of this century. Some became extremely rich and inevitably excited the envy of the Malays. Yet the Chinese, sundered by dialect and clan, lacked a common voice which would gain them political influence. They were unanimous only in refusing to integrate. The Islam of the native Malays posed a formidable barrier to social intercourse, and in any case the Chinese still thought of mainland China as their home, to which they expected to return when they had earned enough to buy a parcel of land or establish a business.

While the Chinese made their fortunes in Malaysia's towns, the British were embarking on a new venture in the countryside—turning the jungle-clad slopes into a parade ground of rubber trees. Progress was slow at first, but after the turn of the century motor vehicles began to ride on rubber tyres and demand soared. The golden years were from 1900 to 1930. Even today, with other commodities gradually replacing rubber, Malaysia has two million hectares of the crop, 60 per cent of all West Malaysia's cultivated ground, and almost two million people depend on it for their livelihood.

Most of the British planters, like the civil servants who administered the protectorate, saw Malaya as only a temporary home. In contrast to the Dutch settlers in Indonesia, many of whom had been there for generations, the British came out to make their careers in their twenties and retired to the mother country in their sixties. During their sojourn in Malaya they worked hard, drank freely and congregated in the local European clubs to play bridge and browse through yellowing newspapers.

Their estate workers, who quickly became skilled at the delicate but tedious task of tapping rubber trees for their latex, were for the most part armies of impoverished Tamils brought over in contract gangs from Madras. These Indians, confined to the rubber plantations by their brutal coolie supervisors, lived in cramped, disease-ridden row tenements and died in obscurity in the malaria-infested jungle.

Other Indians came to the towns and cities of Malaya to man the railways, open sweet shops and teach in the schools. Some of their children bettered themselves and became lawyers and doctors. Though less isolated than the workers locked away on the plantations, the urban Indians remained out of the Malayan mainstream. An intricate structure of snobbery reinforced religious and caste prejudice.

Like the Chinese and Indians, the Malays themselves were a mixed group. The indigenous population had received infusions from Arab and Indian Muslim traders, from Thai and Borneo blood lines and also from 20th-century migrants from Indonesia. The traditional designation of Malays as *bumiputras* was becoming a very rough approximation when so many of the Malays were first-generation immigrants from thousands of kilometres away. As blood became less significant in the definition of a Malay, so three other factors grew in importance: the Malay language, the religion of Islam and devotion to the nine sultans.

The British, far more than the Dutch in Indonesia, were careful to support the Malay race, not only in cultivating the favours of the native aristocracy but also in protecting Islam from alien influences. Residents were often men knowledgeable in local languages and customs. Some Malays received a Western-style education from the British and secured junior jobs in the civil service. The Chinese and Indians, in contrast, were kept out of the administration. With such patronage as evidence, the British could claim to be the one force that protected Malay integrity in the face of the flood of immigrants. Malays at every level accepted them as such and

A coach winds its way through a tea plantation in the Cameron Highlands—a tract of forested hills in the centre of West Malaysia. The Highlands are a popular venue for tourists drawn by the temperate climate and panoramic views.

did not later turn against the sultans for collaborating with the colonial power. When independence came, it would find the Malay people economically weak in comparison with the Chinese, but far stronger politically, thanks to the rallying power of their religion and their rulers.

There was little call for independence in the early decades of the 20th century; it took the Second World War to sharpen aspirations. The war began for Malaysia late in 1941, when Japanese invaders swept through the ill-defended country in 55 days. Sarawak and North Borneo fell to Japan in February 1942. About 70,000 British military and civilians were captured and interned, most of them in Singapore.

During their four-year occupation, the Japanese treated Malaysians in markedly different ways depending on their race. The new masters were placatory to the Indians, whom they hoped would join Japanese-sponsored anti-British armies. With the Malays, the policy was more ambiguous: discipline was strict but the position of the sultans was left undisturbed. The real victims of the invasion were the Chinese, who were treated savagely.

Eventually, the cruelty of the occupation forces, the hunger and deprivation experienced by all races and the threat of forced labour on the Burmese railway turned not just the Chinese but also the others against the Japanese. But the defeat of the British in 1941 had broken the spell of white domination. In 1945, the British returned to Malaysia hoping to usher in a new colonial era. They created a Crown Colony out of the Federated and Unfederated Malay States together with Penang and Malacca; Sarawak and North Borneo became Crown Colonies

3

too. It was soon clear, however, that their days were numbered.

The trigger for an Independence movement was a plan put forward by London in 1946 for a new form of colonial administration for the peninsula. In this proposed "Malayan Union", all races would hold essentially the same rights. The project immediately ran into opposition from the hitherto docile Malays, who were indignant at the ideas of parity. Already feeling increasingly "strangers in their own land", as one slogan put it, the Malays formed a political party, the United Malays' National Organization, to put their case for special treatment. The sultans wavered, and then threw their weight against the plan. Faced with united Malay opposition, the British went back to their committees and over the next two years a more acceptable formula emerged. The British, however, were still thinking in terms of a self-governing colony, while the newly politicized Malays—and increasingly the Chinese and Indians—began pressing for self-rule to be taken to its logical conclusion: Independence.

Independence for Malaya might have come sooner than it did had not the wartime anti-Japanese guerrilla fighters of the Malayan Communist Party (MCP) tried to take over the government by force. Officially designated as an "Emergency", the bitter guerrilla conflict that began in 1948 lasted 12 years. A key technique of the guerrillas, the vast majority of whom were ethnic Chinese, was to attack isolated plantations and police stations from jungle sanctuaries. Among 2,500 civilian victims, the Malay Communist Party succeeded in ambushing and killing the British High Commissioner, Sir Henry Gurney, and for many years no planter went out of his home without a weapon.

By degrees, the British eliminated guerrilla activity from peninsular Malaysia except in the far north, partly by mounting military attacks, partly by removing rural Chinese—who would otherwise have supplied the fighters—to new villages well clear of the action. As the guerrilla fighters lost ground, the morale of the MCP weakened. It had never been supported by the Malay peasantry or most of the Indian estate workers, and eventually it lost Chinese backing too. By the mid-1950s most of the rebels had either surrendered or been captured, though it was not until 1960, three years into Independence, that the state of emergency was declared at an end. The MCP has never surrendered, however. Today its much depleted forces operate from underground bases in the difficult terrain just north of the Malaysian-Thai border and a few hundred still roam around inside West Malaysia.

By the mid-1950s, when the British had contained the guerrilla threat, they recognized that they would have to heed the demands for independence. Empires were crumbling fast. The French had already left South-East Asia; the Portuguese still held East Timor and the Dutch Irian Jaya, but the British colonies were the last of real importance in the region. Having stamped out Communism, the colonial authorities felt confident that they would be handing the country over to reliable heirs. Negotiations on a Constitution for an independent Malaya began in earnest.

The British would not budge on equal citizenship rights for all races; by now it had become clear to everyone that the Chinese and the Indians were in Malaya to stay. Mao Tse-tung had declared the People's Republic of China in 1949, and the majority of Malaya's Chinese were prepared neither to live under a Communist regime nor to forego the economic advantages they had built for themselves. For the first time, they saw Malaya as home and looked forward to full membership in an independent nation.

The British were, however, forced by the strength of Malay feeling to entrench "special privileges" for the Malays in the Constitution. Enormous tracts of agricultural land were reserved for Malays, and they were granted preferential access to jobs in the civil service. Malay was recognized as the national language and Islam was designated the state religion, to be used on formal state occasions. This was not to mean, though, that Malaysia would become an Islamic state, in which Islamic law would apply to all inhabitants. Although the Constitution defined a Malay as, among other things, a person who "embraces Islam", the other races were guaranteed freedom of worship. The nine sultanates were retained and a unique rotating kingship was established. Each of the nine royal houses was to hold the kingship for five years in turn.

The delicate negotiations over the Malay privileges were completed in June 1957, and two months later the Independence of Malaya was announced. It became a federal democracy composed of 11 states—the nine sultanates plus the former Straits Settlements of Malacca and Penang.

Hardly had Malaya achieved independence when Singapore, then still a British Crown Colony, proposed a merger with its larger neighbour. In the early 1960s, the scope of the plan

A CHRONOLOGY OF KEY EVENTS

c. 3000 B.C. The first of two waves of Malay peoples from southern China reaches the Malay Peninsula and the islands beyond. The second wave arrives around 300 B.C.

c. 100–1450 A.D. The peninsula is divided among many small trading states, whose religion is a mixture of Hinduism and Buddhism brought from India.

c. 1403–1511 Malacca becomes the foremost city-state in the peninsula. After a Muslim ruler ascends the throne, taking the title of Sultan, Islam spreads through the region.

1511 Under Affonso d'Albuquerque, a famous Portuguese navigator (*below*), the Portuguese conquer the city-state of Malacca.

1641 The Dutch take Malacca from Portugal. Sultanates elsewhere on the peninsula gain strength.

1786 The British East India Company acquire the island of Penang from the Sultan of Kedah.

1824 The Dutch cede Malacca to the British.

1826 Britain starts to administer Penang, Malacca and Singapore as a single unit—the Straits Settlements.

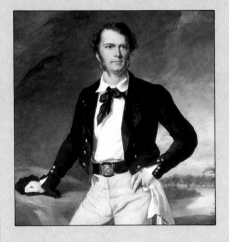

1840 The English adventurer James Brooke (*above*) quells a rebellion in Sarawak against its overlord, the Sultan of Brunei. As a reward, he is made Rajah of Sarawak in 1841. His descendants will rule until 1946.

1848–1900 Tens of thousands of Chinese migrate into the Malay Peninsula to work as tin miners.

1874 Following unrest among the Chinese, two sultanates agree to accept British Residents to guide the sultans in government. Over the next few decades, British advisors are installed in other sultanates (*below*).

1881 The British North Borneo Company is granted a Royal Charter to administer a large territory previously under the Sultan of Brunei.

1896 A federal government for Malaya is established in Kuala Lumpur.

c. 1900 Malayan plantations begin to grow rubber on a large scale. Indian labourers are brought in to tap the trees. By 1920, Malaya produces more than half the world's rubber.

1941–1942 The Japanese invade Malaya, Sarawak and North Borneo.

1945 British rule returns to Malaya.

1946 The United Malays' National Organization (UMNO) is founded to campaign for Malay rights.

1946 Sarawak and North Borneo become British Crown Colonies.

1948 Chinese Communists in Malaya organize guerrilla resistance against British rule. The British declare a state of emergency, which does not end until 1960.

1957 Britain grants independence to the Federation of Malaya. The first prime minister is Tunku Abdul Rahman.

1963 The Federation of Malaysia is created. It includes Malaya, Sarawak, Singapore and North Borneo, now renamed Sabah (*coat of arms above*).

1965 Singapore leaves the federation.

1969 Serious race riots lead to the suspension of parliamentary rule for nearly two years.

1980 Petroleum, mainly from Sarawak, takes the place of rubber as Malaysia's chief export.

3

was further enlarged to include the other British Crown Colonies, Sarawak and North Borneo, together with the sultanate of Brunei, which was a British protectorate. Eventually Brunei, unwilling to share its ample oil revenues, declined to join the union. North Borneo and Sarawak, though initially fearful of a new form of colonialism, were won over with a number of concessions: indigenous people would enjoy the same privileges as peninsular Malays and funds would be set aside for the states' economic development.

In 1963, the Federation of Malaysia, consisting of Malaya, Singapore, Sarawak and North Borneo—now renamed Sabah—was proclaimed. In 1965, unhappy about the entrenched position of the Malays, Singapore went its separate way and Malaysia assumed the shape it has today.

It is a rare example of a Third World country that has remained faithful to the form of democracy bequeathed to it by its departing colonial ruler. Each of the 13 states—the original 11 plus Sarawak and Sabah—has its own elected assembly. The leader of the party or coalition that dominates in the elections becomes chief minister and nominates the state's executive council. In the nine states which have sultans, the sultan is the titular head of the state, but the executive council is responsible to the state assembly rather than to the sultan. The powers of the states are not great: they control land laws, Muslim and Malay customary laws, agriculture, and some aspects of social welfare and local government. Sarawak and Sabah, as part of the incentive to join the Malaysian union, were granted a little more autonomy than the others. Notably, they wield authority over immigration, including that of

A multi-storey office block strikes a jarring note in Kuala Lumpur's green and tranquil suburb of Bukit Bintang. Such oases of gracious living, once a hallmark of the capital, are giving way to high-density estates erected to house the fast-growing urban population.

Malaysian citizens from other states, thus ensuring that the *bumiputras* will retain their numerical dominance.

At the federal level, where the real power lies, there are many echoes of the British system. The king is head of state but without day-to-day executive power; he may act to dissolve parliament but otherwise his role is largely ceremonial. Parliament consists of two houses. Some of the Senate—the upper chamber—are elected by the state assemblies; the majority are chosen by the prime minister from among the nation's most eminent men. Members of the lower chamber, the House of Representatives, are directly elected. The Senate has more real power than Britain's House of Lords but money bills are processed only by the House of Representatives. The cabinet must all be members of parliament and the prime minister—the government's chief executive officer—is, as in Britain, the leader of the dominant party.

The federal government wields authority over defence, law and order, finance, education, health, communications and labour affairs. The states are largely dependent on the federal government for allocations of funds, and in consequence their scope for manoeuvre is limited. Relations with central government are harmonious when the same party is in power at both levels, but otherwise conflicts can arise; they are almost invariably resolved in favour of the federal government. These occasional tensions have not been severe enough to damage the structure: elections are fair, *coups d'état* are unheard-of and the military stays clear of politics.

One of the first priorities of the leaders of independent Malaysia was to de-velop the economy. It would have been easy to rely on plantation products and the country's abundant natural resources—huge tin deposits, major reserves of both oil and natural gas, commercial quantities of coal, iron ore, bauxite, gold and manganese, and great tracts of forest yielding tropical hardwoods. But Malaysians were well aware that the colonial economy based on tin and rubber had tied their country to London commerce and had denied it the resilience that a spread of industries or even a local processing capacity would have given. Soon after Independence, the politicians decided to lessen dependence on commodities by diversifying into manufacturing.

A lot of government money and an increasingly large slice of the country's growing national debt was staked on the success of large, heavy industry projects, among them pig-iron production, shipyards, cement plants and engineering complexes. Malaysia began to export electronic components and textiles. Recently, it has even become an automobile manufacturer, in a joint venture with Japan's Mit-subishi Motor Corporation. Today, manufactures bring in about a quarter of Malaysia's export earnings.

Malaysia feels somewhat hampered in its drive to industrialize by its small population. Almost alone among developing nations, it has resolved to encourage procreation, chiefly to create a bigger domestic market and a larger work force. Government ministers' exhortations to women to stay at home and raise children make the Chinese and Indians uneasy, since the Malays remain a largely rural people and, like farmers everywhere, tend to rear large families. Any boost in the population in the near future is likely to increase the proportion of Malays in the population and push it over 50 per cent.

Nonetheless, Malaysia's population problems are minor compared to its neighbours'. Though the need for more workers is a matter for concern, it is far more manageable than an excessively large number of mouths to feed—the trouble in most of South-East Asia. Besides, Malaysian workers make up in educational attainments what they lack in numbers. In particular, the

Chinese are legendary for their fierce drive to educate their families. The government has played its part in spreading skills, regularly budgeting at least 15 per cent of its annual expenditure on education. Malaysians support six universities, several with branch campuses around the country.

The move to industrialize has left 30 per cent of Malaysians still on the land. Many Malay smallholders have turned in the past few decades from subsistence rice growing to rubber cultivation. In the rubber and oil palm plantations of West Malaysia, the majority of workers are still Indians. Trade-union agitation has greatly improved their lot, but conditions of near-slavery still occasionally come to light. Across the water in underpopulated Sabah, where many plantations have been started since the 1970s, the workers are mainly migrant labourers from the Philippines and Indonesia.

Jobs in mining are dwindling as world demand for tin shrinks. But the key place of tin in the economy has been taken by oil and gas, which became a major revenue-spinner in the 1970s. Today, output is about half that of energy-rich Indonesia. There are some deposits off the eastern shore of West Malaysia and others in the seas north of Sabah, but the largest reserves are off Sarawak. Sarawak and Sabah see only 5 per cent of their substantial oil revenues; the rest passes straight into the federal government's coffers.

Thanks to its natural riches and the energy of its people, Malaysia has been one of Asia's post-Independence success stories. Increases in national products mounted steadily in the 1960s, reaching 4 per cent per annum by the end of the decade. Accelerating growth continued during the 1970s, helped by a commodities boom and burgeoning world trade. By 1980, growth rates were up to nearly 9 per cent a year.

But unfortunately for the continuing health of the economy, the country's bureaucracy grew almost as fast as its GDP. Malaysia's federal system, in which central government departments' efforts are often replicated at state level, absorbs more than the normal complement of under-employed civil servants. The nation has consequently acquired ASEAN's highest proportion of public-sector workers.

Moreover, Malaysia remains rather more dependent on commodities than it would like. A simultaneous dip in world prices for tin, rubber and palm oil in the mid-1980s jolted growth rates down by several notches and

TAPPING THE POTENTIAL OF RUBBER

At dawn, when the latex is flowing most freely, a plantation worker taps a rubber tree by the light of a candle (*below*). After collection, the latex is mixed with formic acid to make it coagulate; then it is washed and squeezed between rollers and hung up to dry (*right*).

More than half of Malaysia's cultivated land is given over to rubber, yet a century ago not a single rubber plant grew in the country. Natives of Brazil, the trees were introduced to the peninsula by H. N. Ridley, an English botanist who also developed techniques for growing them intensively on plantations.

The development of the automobile industry in the early 20th century guaranteed the success of the enterprise by creating a huge demand for rubber. After World War II, growers began to face competition from synthetic substitutes. Yet by developing more prolific strains, they helped Malaysia maintain its position as the world's chief supplier of the natural product, currently meeting one third of global demand.

strengthened governmental resolve to diversify the economy still further.

The new wealth has not been shared equally by all Malaysians. The Chinese remain the richest group overall, paramount in the financial and service sectors. Many of them operate on an international scale, with interests in Singapore and Hong Kong as well as at home. They enjoy their wealth discreetly, ploughing much of it back into the business if it is their own, and lavishing funds on their children's education. Family ties are strong and the continuity of the business through successive generations matters keenly.

One of the most respected Chinese businessmen is Tun Tan Siew Sin, scion of a family established in Malacca since the early 18th century. Tan's wealthy father took care not to spoil his only son when he was a child, and impressed on him the virtues of hard work and financial prudence. After a career in politics that culminated in a 15-year spell as finance minister in the 1960s and early 1970s, Tan entered the corporate world at its highest level by becoming chairman of Sime Darby, ASEAN's largest company. Under Tan, Sime Darby diversified from its traditional speciality, plantations, into car sales, computer software marketing and commodity trading. An astute operator who could more than hold his own in any circle of world financiers, Tan attributed part of his success to the understanding of his fellow-countrymen that his long roots in their soil have given him.

But many Chinese made their fortunes without the benefit of Tan's background. Teh Hong Piow, the richest banker in Malaysia, is the son of a salesman born in Swatow, a city in China's Kwangtung province. Teh himself was born in Singapore, where he began his career as a bank clerk; he only moved to Malaysia in 1960. Six years later, at the age of 36, he became the youngest-ever holder of a banking licence, and by the mid-1980s his institution, Public Bank, was the largest privately owned bank in Malaysia.

At the opposite end of the scale, many Chinese are undeniably poor; some scrape a living as tailors, others as hawkers or small farmers. But overall, the Chinese are comfortably off compared with the Indians, many of whom still languish on the plantations. The Malays, starting from a level far below that of the Chinese, have made the most dramatic gains of all, consolidating and extending the advantages they secured at the time of Independence. They have a good way to go before they catch up with the Chinese, but they now control many commanding heights of the economy, including plantation and manufacturing companies, banks and commercial ventures. On the whole, the successful Malays live more ostentatiously than the Chinese. They buy opulent cars and expensive clothes and indulge in frequent trips abroad. Many make the pilgrimage to Mecca more than once, and have apartments in London.

One of the wealthiest *bumiputra* businessmen is Syed Kechik, who has interests in property development, banking and television. He dropped out of school at the age of 13 to become a street hawker but caught up later; aged 18, he took a job as a seaman on a boat bound for California and continued his formal education on his arrival in the United States, eventually acquiring a degree in political science. After training as a barrister in London, he returned to Malaysia and became a noted lawyer and political adviser. From this prominent vantage point he launched himself in business.

Syed Kechik is typical among Malay businessmen in using politics as a starting point for a business career. The normal procedure is to build a network of contacts through politics, then apply for a government licence to import or manufacture some items. Tan notwithstanding, the Chinese business community is much more likely to remain at arm's length from politics, though many of them have found it advisable to bring Malays with useful connections on to their boards.

The Malays as a community have won most of their recent advantages through the ballot box. Like most Malaysians, the Malays vote for parties organized on rigidly ethnic lines. Since

At a tin mine near the west coast of West Malaysia, a worker breaks up the earth with a high-pressure water jet. The slurry will be pumped to a plant that separates ore from gravel. After 1,500 years of extraction, Malaysia is still the world's largest producer of tin.

they are the largest racial group and the rural districts where they tend to live are disproportionately represented electorally, they are sure of the largest faction in the federal parliament and in most state assemblies. Their principal mouthpiece is the United Malays' National Organization (UMNO); the smaller communities are represented by the Malaysian Chinese Association and the Malaysian Indian Congress, while a number of other parties represent subsections of racial groups.

Yet despite the racial loyalties displayed, Malaysian politics are less divisive than they might appear at first sight. Though squabbles between the races were allowed free play in the federation's early years, since 1970 a coalition of the three main parties and some of the smaller ones has held power at the federal level. Similar coalitions run most of the state governments. The arrangement has generally worked well. In South-East Asian fashion, everyone feels more comfortable searching for consensus within a broad-based government than with the confrontational politics of the West.

The coalitions have, nonetheless, not been a partnership of equals. The UMNO is without doubt the supreme arbiter of policy, strengthened as it is not only by its large constituency but also by old rivalries leading to infighting within the Chinese and Indian parties. The Malay party has provided the prime minister and all senior cabinet members since Independence.

The acquiescence of both the Chinese and Indian communities in the UMNO's continued preponderance stems at least in part from the fears generated by serious race riots in May 1969. Their main underlying cause was the Malays' resentment of Chinese

wealth. The riots followed a Chinese-dominated party's victory in several cities in the 1969 general elections. Chauvinist sentiments overflowed, and crowds spilled out of Malay areas in Kuala Lumpur to burn and loot and kill; Chinese and Indian shopkeepers defended themselves and retaliated. The troubles lasted for several days. Among hundreds killed were representatives of every race, but the Chinese and Indian communities suffered the worst casualties. The government responded by imposing martial law and suspending parliament. A National Operations Council took over running the country for almost two years.

Although parliamentary rule was resumed in 1971, it is now recognized that 1969 was a pivotal date for post-Independence Malaysia, holding the same emotive power as 1965 for Indonesians. The temporary government was dominated by *bumiputras*, and it responded to the riots by taking steps that would dramatically increase the Malays' stake in the economy. As soon as parliamentary rule was reimposed, the native race's special privileges were strengthened by legislation that made questioning of Malay prerogatives a seditious act. Though an under-

standable reaction against their former economic hardships, the changes the Malays pushed through parliament made the Chinese and Indians politically second-class citizens.

The shift in emphasis is epitomized by the difference in outlook between the two leading Malay politicians of the past few decades. Tunku Abdul Rahman, often fondly referred to as "the father of Malaysia", became the country's first prime minister in 1957 and retained his position for 13 years. Though a member of a Malay royal family—he was the 21st son of the 25th Sultan of Kedah—he eschewed a narrowly Malay outlook. While accepting that each race in the country wanted to retain its own identity, he insisted that "there is too much talk about differences and not enough about our similarities". Indeed, he carried his commitment to a multiracial society into his own family, adopting a Chinese daughter and two Malay sons.

Mahathir Mohamad, who became prime minister in 1981, is by contrast a committed Malay nationalist. He first rose to prominence in the aftermath of the 1969 riots, when he wrote Tunku Abdul Rahman a long letter criticizing his administration for failing to uplift the *bumiputra* population. He was one of the first to demand a radical change in the treatment of the Malays, and he wanted to go further than other politicians. Tunku Abdul Rahman sacked Mahathir from the UMNO and he subsequently lost his parliamentary seat. During his spell in the political wilderness, Mahathir wrote a book called *The Malay Dilemma*, which criticized Malays for demanding privileges without being prepared to work for them. When he finally attained power, Mahathir supported many measures

A sign outside a Penang naval base issues its warning in Malaysia's main languages: Malay, English, Hindi, Tamil, Jawi (Malay in Arabic script) and Mandarin. Although Malay is the official language, many of the Chinese and Indians cannot read it.

to push Malays into the fast track.

Well before Mahathir's rise, his predecessors had already set that process in motion by means of the New Economic Policy—a 20-year plan designed to conquer poverty by 1990 and to narrow the gap between the *bumiputras* and the Chinese. In such questions as education, transfer of assets in companies, buying up of British plantation assets or opening of wilderness land for settlement, it was ordained that *bumiputras* would invariably receive preferential treatment. Large sums of the education budget, for example, were designated to provide scholarships for Malays to study at special residential schools. Companies were directed to employ quotas of *bumiputras* at all levels of management. The target was for *bumiputras* to hold 30 per cent of the overall equity pie, leaving 40 per cent for other Malaysians and 30 per cent for foreigners. As 1990

drew closer, the target proved unrealistic, but the Malays did succeed in substantially narrowing the gap.

The display of Malay assertiveness has extended beyond economic matters to touch every aspect of national life and to put other races on the defensive. The language issue, for example, which has been the subject of heated debate since Independence, was profoundly affected by the new political climate. The 1969 riots gave impetus to plans to introduce compulsory Malay-language teaching at secondary level in all state schools, a plan progressively implemented over 13 years, reaching university level by 1983.

Other languages show no sign, however, of disappearing. At the primary level, parents still have the option of sending their children to Chinese, Tamil or English vernacular schools. To supplement the Malay-language secondary and university teaching,

many parents employ either English or Chinese-language tutors. Others send their children overseas: by the mid-1980s, 27,000 Malaysians—the majority Chinese—had study places in the United States alone, and many thousands more attended universities and business schools in Australia, Britain, New Zealand and Canada. And despite heavy pressure to substitute Malay, English is still the means of communication in law courts, corporate boardrooms, hospitals and university common rooms, and a neutral language in which people of different races often choose to converse.

The Muslim faith has seen a resurgence in Malaysia that has synchronized with the expanding role of the Malay language. The Malays have always taken Islam more seriously than most Indonesians, whom they view as being rather laggard in their Muslim duties and errant in devotion.

3

Indonesians, in their turn, find Malaysians embarrassingly pious and the religious atmosphere pervading their country stifling. The gap has widened in recent years. To an extent that baffles the Indonesians, Malay culture increasingly seeks inspiration from the worldwide Islamic community. Malay girls, for example, now often cover their hair with light headdresses. Until forbidden by the government in 1985, some women civil servants and university students even adopted the full, black purdah native to the Middle East, which covers all but the eyes. International Koran-reading contests draw the crowds to Kuala Lumpur's gleaming new Islamic Centre, whose austere, pointed arches reflect Middle Eastern inspiration; they contrast abruptly with the more eclectic architecture of earlier religious buildings.

In recent years, Islam has become increasingly politicized. The Partai Islam SaMalaysia, the country's Islamic party, rapidly gained electoral support among Malays in the 1970s. To meet the challenge head-on, the moderate UMNO decided in 1984 to describe itself also as an Islamic party. For justification it could point to the constitutional clause that equates being Malay with being a Muslim. To gain some Islamic credentials, the UMNO-dominated government spent millions to establish an International Islamic University near Kuala Lumpur. It has also sent hundreds of civil servants on seminars to discuss ways of instilling Islamic values into the administration. Although such steps have been taken partly to head off more extreme Islamic movements, non-Muslims are deeply suspicious of them.

Religion underpins the traditional function of the nine sultans who, despite some predictions to the contrary, show no signs of being left behind by Malaysia's rapid industrial and social changes. Malays remain grateful for the sultans' role in securing Malay privileges in the Constitution, and value the link with the past which they represent. The myths and much of the prestige surrounding the sultans have gradually withered over the years, but pomp and extravagance still survive. Their regalia—sacred kris swords, ancient drums and clarionets—are accorded reverence; on state occasions the sultans continue to dress in royal yellow, and a yellow umbrella, a pre-Islamic symbol of authority, surmounts their royal persons.

Their official prerogatives include regulating Malay's religious duties. In some states their strict interpretation of Islamic law has led to the arrest of adulterers, unmarried couples and widows living with non-Muslims. Sultans also have the discretion to award titles and honours, for which all Malaysians share a mania. And many insist on being consulted when sizeable land concessions are being negotiated. Since land sales and rentals are nowadays the major independent source of funds for state governments, which must otherwise rely on the federal government for finance, the involvement of the sultans in land deals gives them a modicum of real power.

They do not entirely conform to the dutiful constitutional role played by the monarchs of such nations as Japan and Britain, and their numbers make them a force to be reckoned with. "There are about 25 monarchs left in the world," a recent Malaysian prime minister commented ruefully, "and half of them are in Malaysia." A few of them enjoy treating chief ministers as mere courtiers and consider themselves above the law.

In the late 1970s, a number of sultans seriously abused their relations with their state governments. Although the Constitution stated that they must assent to bills passed by state assemblies, it gave no time limit; the Sultans of Johore and Perak, both due to become king in the course of the 1980s, used delaying tactics to ease state ministers out of office. Concerned lest even graver iniquities be perpetrated at federal level when one or other of these headstrong leaders was installed as king, the federal government passed a bill in 1983 which would oblige the rulers at both federal and state level to give their assent to legislation within 15 days. The move brought Malaysia close to a constitutional crisis. The King refused to sign the amendment to the Constitution, which all the sultans saw as a grave slur on their dignity.

Eventually a compromise was worked out. The King was granted the right to send a bill back to parliament once for reconsideration, after which he was obliged to sign it promptly. The sultans gave a verbal undertaking not to intervene in state politics: their honour was saved but they had learnt their lesson. In 1984, the Sultan of Johore ascended the Malaysian throne. Despite the federal government's earlier fears, he restricted his public role to that laid down by the Constitution.

Although the continued existence of the sultans serves as a reminder of the strength of Malay culture in multiracial Malaysia, their popularity is not confined to Malays. Recently the sultans have won unexpected support from non-Malays who are unhappy about the prospect of too much power

concentrated in the politicians' hands.

The masters of the new Malaysia have never apologized for their ready use of security legislation. The government's powers include wide discretion to declare localized states of emergency, to detain persons without trial or to try them in camera, to license publications and to forbid gatherings of more than seven people. The evils the government cites in justification of such measures are the threat posed by Communist insurgency, the dangers of religious extremism and drug abuse. The first is well in hand now, but religion remains an explosive issue and the drug problem is serious. Malaysia is on the smuggling route whereby heroin grown in Burma reaches the West. The country's increasingly wealthy youths—many of them disorientated by the rapid social change brought about by economic growth—have turned in large numbers to narcotics, and Malaysia now has 400,000 addicts. To contain the problem, the death penalty is imposed for trafficking, and possession of certain amounts of drugs, including marijuana, constitutes legal proof of guilt.

Despite what many people see as an excessively harsh response to social maladies, constitutionally guaranteed liberties make Malaysia a freer place than most of its neighbours. The country's complicated federalism accommodates its diversity, allowing an impressive pluralism of thought, religious persuasion and political affinity.

Malaysia's plural society is seen at its best on traditional holidays—the Chinese New Year, the Hindu festival of Deepavali, and Hari Raya, the Islamic celebration of the end of the fasting month. For Hari Raya, the country's Muslims, from the prime minister to paddy labourer, receive neighbours and guests of every race. Spicy Malay stews and salads are placed on long tables and from morning to dusk, often for several days in a row, lines of visitors help themselves. It is an occasion for patching up old quarrels and for asking forgiveness, for reflections on the year past and resolutions for the future. The conversation is light but touches on matters most central to Malaysians, Muslim or non-Muslim.

At Chinese New Year and Deepavali, it is the other races' turn to be the hosts. Again, the disparate strands of a complex nation draw together in a spirit of tolerance and amity.

THE SINGAPORE SUCCESS STORY

In January 1819, Sir Stamford Raffles, a high official of Britain's East India Company, sailed the South China Sea in search of a suitable site for a trading settlement which could be developed into "a great commercial emporium and a fulcrum whence we may extend our influence politically". His quest ended on a diamond-shaped, predominantly flat island at the tip of the Malay Peninsula, about a kilometre from the mainland and just one degree north of the equator. Its name was Singapura, "Lion City"—acquired, according to legend, after a 12th-century Sumatran prince encountered on its shores a black-faced tiger which he mistakenly identified as a lion.

Ostensibly, Singapore was an improbable choice for Raffles to make. The island was almost entirely covered by dense jungle and mosquito-infested mangrove swamps. It was inhabited only by a few hundred Malay fishermen and traders, and a considerably greater number of tigers and crocodiles. According to Raffles, the banks of its principal river were strewn with hundreds of skulls belonging to the victims of pirates. In its favour, however, were excellent deep-water anchorage and natural harbours on its southern shore; moreover, it was located half way along the principal trading route between India and China. Commanding an entrance to the Indian Ocean, the South China Sea and the Java Sea, it was strategically placed to become

the main entrepôt of South-East Asia.

Today, Raffles' phrase "a great commercial emporium" admirably describes the independent city-state of Singapore. The island, a mere 618 square kilometres in area, is approximately twice as large as the similarly shaped Isle of Wight, and less than one fifth the size of Rhode Island. It has no natural resources besides its harbour and the considerable enterprise of its 2.5 million population. Yet the island is a major financial, industrial and communications centre, as well as a key staging post in the transport of commodities, especially for oil from Indonesia and rubber and tin from Malaysia. It has become the world's second busiest port, after Rotterdam; it is also South-East Asia's largest petroleum-refining centre, largest container port and largest shipbuilding and repair centre. Every year, its port handles more than a 100 billion dollars' worth of trade and is used by more than 300 international shipping lines. Every month, its modernistic palace of an airport handles about 700,000 passengers and some 22,000 tonnes of air cargo.

In the course of a year, Singapore attracts more tourists than it numbers inhabitants—primarily because it is a duty-free paradise for shoppers and gourmets. Whether their taste is for antique Chinese porcelain or for the latest electronic equipment, crocodile-skin handbags or designer shirts, snake

Named after the founder of Singapore, the century-old Raffles Hotel preserves the graciousness of colonial days in its classical façades and immaculate greenery. Behind it rises Raffles City, an ultramodern skyscraper complex which includes one of the world's tallest hotels.

4

steak or French cuisine, Singapore fulfils their desires.

Thanks to its commercial success, Singapore has the highest standard of living in Asia after Brunei and Japan. Indeed, its per capita income is higher than those of Greece and Spain. Virtually the whole population enjoys a share in the prosperity: Singapore has few slums, almost no beggars, minimal unemployment and a life expectancy of 75 for women and 70 for men. By most criteria, it is a developed nation.

Physically, this dynamic state bears little resemblance to the island where Raffles landed. Throughout Singapore, tropical forest has given way to concrete jungle, relieved by manicured oases of greenery and crisscrossed by over 3,000 kilometres of highways bordered with grass and flowering shrubs. The towering office blocks and sumptuous hotels, the flyovers, cable cars and drive-in theatres, are all thoroughly Western in style. In the harbour, the sampans and junks of local traders are far outnumbered by giant supertankers and container ships.

There are still a few Malay *kampongs*, villages of stilt houses thatched with palm leaves and surrounded by fruit trees. But more than 70 per cent of Singapore's population now lives in 10 and 20-storey apartment blocks that are subsidized by the government. The blocks are built in clusters to form self-contained mini-towns with their own shopping precincts, cinemas, playgrounds and community centres. For many years, Singapore has maintained a construction rate of one new living unit every 17 minutes. Singapore's phenomenal expansion even creates new living space out of the ocean. Since the 1960s, the land area has grown by some 36 square kilometres as

Poles of washing and vigorous weeds sprout from the upper floors of decrepit Chinese tenements. A few streets of such buildings have been preserved as tourist attractions, but most of Singapore's old dwellings have been razed to the ground and replaced by concrete tower blocks.

a result of ambitious reclamation projects that dredge up soil from the sea.

Malays have long since ceased to be the dominant ethnic group. Singapore's population is 76 per cent ethnic Chinese, 15 per cent Malay and 7 per cent Indian, with minorities of Eurasians and other groups. Near the main port area in the south-west, there is a Chinatown, with narrow winding lanes congested with barrow traders and flanked by two-storey shophouses; around Serangoon Road in the north of the city, Indians in saris and dhotis predominate. But the Chinese and Indians, like the Malays, have largely been rehoused in apartment blocks, with the result that the old racial communities are breaking down.

A confusing babel of languages prevails. Hakka, Hokkien and Cantonese dialects of Chinese are heard on the streets, and there are in addition four official tongues—Mandarin, English, Malay and Tamil—in which all official documents are published. English is increasingly the lingua franca; it is the main language of business, government and education. But Malay, being the language of the indigenous people, receives special mention in the Constitution: the government is enjoined to safeguard and foster it.

Culturally, too, Singapore is eclectic. There are Hindu temples, Muslim mosques, Buddhist sanctuaries, Christian cathedrals, Jewish synagogues. *Aficionados* can enjoy such Western pursuits as golf, horse racing, polo and cricket; equally, the city-state offers a wealth of Eastern diversions, including Chinese street opera, snake charmers and an annual Dragon Boat festival.

Near the mouth of the river where he originally landed stands a bronze

A Chinese woman perches barefoot at a public telephone booth. There are about 40 telephones for every 100 Singaporeans—the highest count in Asia outside Japan—and local calls from private installations are free.

statue of the man "to whose foresight and genius Singapore owes its existence and prosperity". It is an unstinting tribute, but hardly more than the city's remarkable founder deserves. Raffles, a self-educated man, joined the East India Company as a clerk and rose rapidly in the hierarchy. At the age of 30 he became Lieutenant-Governor of the Dutch East Indies, when they were occupied by the British in 1811 during the Napoleonic Wars. He instituted many reforms to improve the conditions of the native population—so many that his superiors, alarmed at the expenses he was incurring, recalled him. Undaunted, Raffles sought an alternative base for British interests and focused his choice on the island of Singapore.

Within one week of sighting his future metropolis, Raffles negotiated British right of settlement in return for regular annual payments to the island's territorial chief and to his overlord, the Sultan of Johore. In 1824, under the terms of a new treaty, the

main island, together with 54 adjacent islets, was ceded outright to Britain.

Before the advent of Singapore the Dutch had monopolized trade in the region. Raffles made Singapore a free port, and his move rapidly destroyed the Dutch hold. In 1825, Singapore's trade was worth £2.5 million. Forty years later, it had expanded sixfold. At the end of the century, Malaya's great tin and rubber booms brought new wealth to Singapore.

The prosperous island needed far more labour than could be supplied by the indigenous Malay population. Malays migrated to the island from the mainland and from Indonesia; Indians came as traders and labourers; and large numbers of Chinese indentured labourers were also brought in. The first census of 1824 showed a population of nearly 11,000, with the Malays in the majority, but by 1860 more than 60 per cent of the population was Chinese. By 1911, when Singapore passed the quarter-million mark, the Chinese made up nearly three quarters of the population—a proportion maintained to the present day.

In the heyday of the British Empire, the cosmopolitan port of Singapore represented a haven of civilization to the expatriate rubber planters of Malaya. Their favourite haunt was the Raffles Hotel, which survives to this day. Though now considerably modernized and enlarged, it preserves a certain venerable charm with its stuccoed, neoclassical pillars, its huge potted plants, and its celebrated invention, the cocktail known as the Singapore Sling, one half gin, one quarter cherry brandy, one quarter tropical fruit juices, with a dash of Cointreau and Benedictine. During the 1920s and 1930s, the hotel numbered among its

4

numerous distinguished devotees the writer Somerset Maugham, who gathered material for many of his stories from loquacious guests within its walls.

Other than the Raffles Hotel, there are few remaining relics of Singapore's luxurious European sector which, under the British Empire, had contrasted violently with the cramped, vigorous world of Chinatown and the seedy, leisurely paced Indian quarter. Native Singapore was in those days a city of beggars and prostitutes, of sweatshop cottage industries and cut-throat wheeler-dealing. Crime was highly organized and controlled by Mafia-style Chinese secret societies that engaged in open gang warfare. As late as 1932, children could be sold as household slaves and concubines.

The start of World War II in Europe at first made no difference to life in the city-state. Protected by a formidable naval base and a large army garrison, it seemed an impregnable fortress. But, early in the morning of December 8, 1941, Japanese Navy bombers launched an air raid for which the city, still blazing with lights, was totally unprepared. Within days, the news reached Singapore that the Japanese were thrusting southwards through Malaya. Despite this intelligence, General Percival, the Commanding Officer, refused to have Singapore's northern beaches fortified. Batteries of guns still pointed out to sea in the south, in anticipation of a naval attack.

Early in January 1942, air raids were hitting Singapore almost daily, but night after night, in the ballroom of Raffles Hotel, colonials danced on behind blackout blinds and chorused "There'll always be an England". Then, General Archibald Wavell, the new Far East Commander, arrived to impose a belated sense of urgency. He ordered the building of northern fortifications, and the bulk of the British land forces were assembled on the north-east beaches to confront the threat from the mainland. The Japanese launched their invasion on February 8—but on the north-west shore.

They found Singapore hopelessly ill-prepared. A million people were cornered in a city running short of food, water, ammunition and petrol. And so, on February 15, when plans for evacuation by sea were still appallingly confused, General Percival was authorized to surrender. Sir Winston Churchill called it "the worst disaster and largest capitulation in British history". Troops and British civilians alike were consigned to three and a half years in the island's infamous Changi prison camp or as labourers in the jungles of South-East Asia.

Even though the Allies returned in 1945 to liberate Singapore, the great debacle wiped out the mystique of white rule for ever. The cry for independence grew. Britain was slow to heed Singapore's pleas for self-determination, seeing the island as a key strategic outpost and a vital communications centre. Moreover, it was not clear what form independence could take. The colony was so economically dependent on Malaya that the British did not believe it capable of developing into a viable independent state. Nor did they consider that an island with such a formidable Chinese majority could ever exist harmoniously within the framework of a Malay-dominated Federation of Malaysia.

A measure of self-government was granted in 1954. As a result, political activity increased markedly and a number of new parties emerged; the

At Chinese New Year, a group of celebrants manipulate a cloth dragon in pursuit of a pearl. The dragon represents the world's terror, the pearl its beauty; much as the dragon may squirm, it never quite succeeds in swallowing the gem.

4

most notable among them was the vigorous, left-wing People's Action Party (PAP). The demand for further reform grew until, in 1959, Singapore was granted full internal self-government, with Britain retaining control of the island's foreign affairs and defence.

The first elections held under this new Constitution resulted in a massive mandate for the PAP, whose platform included total independence for Singapore and a merger with Malaya. The PAP wanted to become part of a larger unit not only for the sake of political stability, but also for the economic benefits of a large market for the island's developing industries. Singapore joined the Federation of Malaysia at its inception in 1963.

The marriage was not a success. The common market within the federation, which would have benefited Singapore's manufacturers, failed to materialize. And, as many had predicted, Singapore could not reconcile itself to the privileges accorded to Malays in the Malaysian Constitution. Singapore had hoped that Malaysia would relax its position on race, but the opposite happened: Malays in Malaysia grew alarmed at the increased proportion of Chinese in the enlarged federation. After only two years—a period marked by a variety of disagreements—Singapore agreed to withdraw from the union. On August 9, 1965, it became a sovereign nation.

Having begun its history under the command of one outstanding man, Singapore found another remarkable leader to take it through its first decades of Independence. Lee Kuan Yew was born in 1923, into a wealthy Chinese family in Singapore. Educated at Raffles College (which has since been incorporated into Singapore University) and at Cambridge, he made his mark on the island after World War II as a labour lawyer. In 1954 he became involved in organizing the PAP. Five years later, when Singapore was accorded internal self-government, Lee became the nation's first prime minister. He was to remain at the helm for more than a quarter of a century.

Noting the PAP's tenacious hold on power, commentators have frequently described Singapore as a "benevolent dictatorship". Among independent Singapore's first acts were measures to curb potential opposition. The government adapted existing British colonial legislation under which any suspected Communists and political opponents of the government could be detained indefinitely without trial, or banished for lengthy periods to nearby islands. Illegal striking was made a prison offence, and no strike was lawful without the backing of a majority of union members through secret ballot, or while the relevant dispute was before the Industrial Arbitration Court.

In the 1968 national elections, the PAP won control of all seats in parliament, a monopoly it maintained until 1981 when Ben Jeyaretnam of the centrist Workers' Party found himself providing a one-man opposition in a 79-member parliament. In the general election three years later, the PAP's share of the vote fell from 75 per cent to 64 per cent, and a second opposition member took his seat in parliament. Otherwise, the power of Lee's administration remained unchallenged for more than two decades.

Officially, Singapore is designated a parliamentary democracy. More than a dozen opposition parties are registered. Elections are held at least every

A 19th-century lithograph, depicting a
presentation to a visiting dignitary in
1846, captures the nucleus of
Singapore and the busy harbour
beyond. Founded only 27 years earlier,
the British settlement had by 1846
acquired some 50,000 inhabitants and
an important slice of the region's trade.

five years, and voting is compulsory for citizens over 21. However, Singapore's democracy has serious limitations. Television and radio are government controlled and no one may publish a newspaper or magazine without an annually renewed government licence. Such constraints limit the opportunities of opposition parties to circulate their viewpoints. The government can call a general election at less than two weeks' notice and the opposition parties, though they may present their policies, are allowed only limited radio and television time.

More significantly, perhaps, the PAP has created the means to ensure that its own ideas permeate Singapore society at every level. All trade union leaders are party members, the majority also being Members of Parliament. Every electoral constituency has a Citizens' Consultative Committee, comprising community leaders who liaise with their parliamentary representative; each neighbourhood has its own sub-committee. The stated purpose of this network is to ensure that the people's needs are channelled upwards to government. But the local representatives have to be approved by the PAP and tend to be apprentices to professional political office. Often the committees control access to government housing and public employment, and dissenters from the PAP line can find themselves discriminated against in the competition for homes and jobs.

Despite the advantages the PAP has granted itself, an overwhelming reaction against it could still be expressed through the ballot box. The party's continuing strength does reflect genuine support—a token of its undeniable achievements, especially in the economic sphere.

Pragmatism has characterized the PAP's approach to the economy from the beginning. In 1959, when Singapore became self-governing, the Western world feared that under a socialist leadership it would be easy prey to creeping Communism in South-East Asia. But Lee recognized that the interests of the island, as a free-trade entrepôt, would not be served by a rejection of capitalist principles. Thus Singapore emerged as a highly unorthodox socialist state: one that encouraged private enterprise and unabashedly championed meritocracy.

Lee's government launched Singapore's industrial revolution in the 1960s by luring foreign investors and multinationals with the bait of tax concessions, cheap and reliable labour, efficient public services and political stability. In the mid-1960s, the government also prepared Singapore for its key position in the financial world when it broke up a cartel of British and local banks that had maintained a stranglehold on high finance in the island. Two Swiss-style concessions—tax exemption for depositors and strict secrecy—subsequently helped make Singapore the "Zurich of the East".

Meanwhile, the government had been financing the multimillion-dollar development of Jurong, a desolate swampland in the south-west which was drained and transformed into a 5,000-hectare industrial estate, with more than 800 factories engaged in making everything from shoelaces to ships. In one decade, with strong emphasis on labour-intensive manufacturing—electronics equipment, light industrial hardware, wood products and textiles—the country's per capita income more than doubled.

Then, in the late 1970s, when Singapore's average annual growth rate of 9.4 per cent was one of the highest in the world, the international oil crisis resulted in developed countries introducing protectionist measures. Lee and his technocrat advisers shrewdly responded by launching Singapore's so-called "second industrial revolution". They switched the emphasis away from labour-intensive to capital-

94

intensive industry and from low-skill to high-technology production, such as advanced electronic components, computer hardware, metal engineering and oil-rig construction. The transformation was achieved chiefly through government loans, tax incentives and help with industrial training for companies prepared to move into the designated sectors. The measures were extremely successful. Between 1979 and 1984, the growth rate averaged more than 8 per cent a year.

In 1985, Singapore's growth rate suddenly dropped below zero. Trade, transport, communications and financial services were still growing, but construction and manufacturing had tumbled; oil refining and electronics were worst hit. Part of the problem was that rises in earnings were beginning to outstrip productivity gains; Singapore was ceasing to be a cheap-labour economy. Malaysia and Indonesia started to compete directly in oil refining and other industries, and Singapore could not keep up.

Characteristically, however, Singaporeans rallied together to combat the decline. Trade unions agreed to forego wage increases. Union officials paraded with placards saying "we sacrifice for national survival", and the National Employers' Association praised the unions for their "responsibility and pragmatism". The government offered a package of concessions to business, including reductions in utilities charges and improvements in Singapore's infrastructure.

At this and the other junctures of Singapore's industrial progress, the government has manipulated the economy indirectly rather than intervening itself. Little industry is in state hands. But, while hardly a typical socialist country in its hands-off approach to business, Singapore offers more welfare benefits and government-funded services than almost any other state in Asia. Its social provisions are much more generous than those of Hong Kong, that other offshore centre of Far Eastern trade and finance.

Singaporeans, for example, enjoy a rudimentary pension system—the only one in Asia outside Japan. Pensions come out of a central provident fund, which builds up from regular contributions made by both employers and employees. The employees may withdraw part of their savings if they are injured or want to buy a government-built apartment. Otherwise they may not remove money from the fund until they retire. In the meantime, the fund provides the government with more than one billion dollars a year for the financing of national development.

But the main thrust of the PAP's socialism has taken the form of massive investment in education, health care and housing. Singapore has the most advanced state-owned and state-subsidized hospitals in South-East Asia, providing medical care for only nominal fees. The public housing system is the envy of many a developed country, with more than seven out of 10 families owning or renting a flat in the clusters of government-built high-rises that have sprung up like great white megaliths across the island.

A first-class education is offered to all children of primary school age. School attendance is still voluntary, but such are the aspirations of the Singaporeans to better their families that primary education is universal. Two thirds of Singapore's children—a higher proportion than in any other ASEAN country—progress to secondary school. Children find themselves in an intensely competitive atmosphere, exacerbated by streaming according to ability at the age of nine. The stress on personal achievement has overlaid many traditional habits of deference and conformity.

Yet, even while Singaporeans are being exhorted to emulate the materialist ambitiousness of the West, they are expected to submit to major government intervention in the direction of their lives. Singapore is a schizophrenic society: dynamic and entrepreneurial, yet retaining much of the respect for government that characterizes other Asian societies. The PAP often acts in a high-handed manner in pursuit of goals that are deemed to be for the ultimate benefit of the people.

In the interests of linguistic homogeneity, for example, the Singapore Broadcasting Corporation has eliminated Chinese dialect broadcasts from its output. It frequently buys Cantonese soap operas from Hong Kong and Taiwan but dubs the sound-tracks in Mandarin before presenting them to its audience—many of whom would understand them far better in Cantonese. The public have, however, found a way round the restricted viewing: they buy special aerials so that their sets can receive dialect transmissions from Malaysia.

But they have no recourse against forcible rehousing, and the price they have paid for their improved living standards is a dismantling of their social milieu. But the destruction of traditional neighbourhoods, besides eliminating slums, has served another of the government's aims: the lowering of barriers between the different races. Ultimately, it is hoped, the diverse

In front of a New York-style skyline, cargo awaits loading at the East Lagoon section of Singapore's vast container port. The island's natural deep-water harbour can provide anchorage for over 400 ships at any one time.

ethnic groups will all but forget their origins and see themselves simply as Singaporeans. The government has grounds for optimism. There is still little intermarriage, but racial tension, which in 1964 erupted in severe riots, is at an all-time low.

To the outsider, particularly one who knew Singapore in its pre-war days, one of the most notable aspects of the new clusters of housing is their cleanliness and tidiness. Singapore generally is the best-ordered city in Asia, largely as a result of strictly enforced legislation. In every neighbourhood the rubbish collector calls seven days a week. Main streets and parks are spotless, thanks to heavy fines for dropping litter or allowing dogs to foul public places, and even the harbour is free of floating rubbish and oil slicks.

With similar efficiency, disease-bearing pests have been almost completely eliminated because it is now an

At a Sunday morning songbird concert, an owner rewards one of the chorus with a titbit. Breeding birds for their voices is a popular and sometimes profitable hobby among Singapore's Chinese; a fine set of vocal chords can raise the value of a pet by several thousand dollars.

offence to leave neglected areas of standing water likely to encourage the procreation of mosquitoes and flies. Early in the 20th century, Singapore had a yearly average of 2,000 deaths from malaria. Now only a few cases of the disease are reported every year. All other tropical diseases have been brought under control. Singapore is one of the few countries in Asia where the tap water is safe to drink. The air, likewise, is wholesome. Smoking is prohibited in many public places and tobacco advertising is banned. There are penalties for emitting excessive smoke from exhaust pipes.

Without doubt, the inspiration for much of the legislation to cleanse the city came from Lee Kuan Yew, an extremely fastidious man known to bathe twice a day, frequently change his shirt, check the temperature of rooms he entered, carefully guard his diet, keep fit with jogging and exercises, and abhor tobacco to such a degree that no Singaporean was permitted to smoke in his presence.

A large and efficient police force ensures that the population adheres to the rules governing hygiene and litter. The police have also scored notable successes in the fight against crime, which dwindled rapidly in the decade following Independence. By the early 1980s, only one Singaporean in 22,000 fell victim to a violent crime in the course of a year, compared with one in 47 New Yorkers. The criminal activity of Chinese secret societies has virtually ceased, and nowhere else in Asia has corruption been brought under greater and more effective control.

The moral wellbeing of Singaporeans is as well protected as their property. Very strict pornography laws pertain: films judged to depict explicit

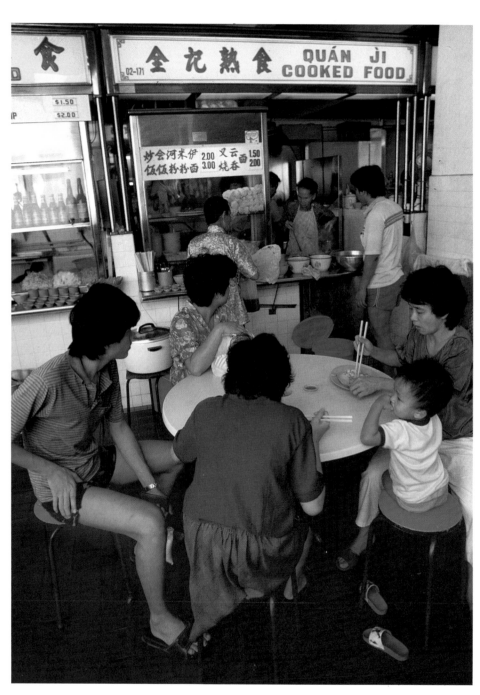

A young family eat out at one of Singapore's innumerable food stalls. At one time, the island was full of open-air snack counters, but now a hygiene-conscious government confines all such cheap fast-food outlets to indoor malls.

4

sex or excessive violence are banned or cut, and tourists have been fined for possession of *Playboy* magazine. Long hair is regarded with suspicion. Government employees have been fined or sacked for wearing their hair over their collars, and many tourists in the late 1960s and early 1970s had to submit to a trim at the airport before they were allowed entry.

More controversially, the Singapore government maintains a strong—some would say intrusive—policy over family planning. The need for a birth control policy became evident soon after Independence. Between 1948 and 1958 Singapore's population had doubled, and by 1965 the annual growth rate was more than 30 per 1,000. The government reacted not only by publicizing birth control methods and making abortion easily available, but also by penalizing large families. The tax relief given for first and second children dropped markedly for a third child, and women received no paid maternity leave on the birth of a fourth. Workers who agreed to be sterilized received an extra week's annual leave.

The campaign was hugely effective: by the early 1980s, the annual birth rate had fallen to 17.3 per 1,000. But by that time the government seemed anxious to influence not merely the number but also the quality of the new generation. In 1983, Lee censured the well-educated youth of Singapore for avoiding or postponing marriage and children in their relentless pursuit of a career and material rewards. Since the less well-educated were more likely to reproduce, a "lopsided pattern of procreating" was emerging. One of the measures introduced to correct the perceived imbalance was a financial inducement for a woman to be steri-lized if the family income and educational attainments were low. But there was so much opposition to this policy that it has since been dropped.

Some observers of Singapore find it so clinically clean and well ordered, so puritanical and repressive, as to be reminiscent of the society depicted in Aldous Huxley's novel *Brave New World*, where social engineering from the womb to the tomb disregards the soul and diminishes human individuality. The same view is expressed in certain circles in Singapore. One university lecturer has written: "One notes a tendency on the part of the government leaders, including the Prime Minister, to view people as digits, buttons to be pressed, gears to be shifted, cogs, units that can be plugged into systems, or beings without moral volition who have to be moved by carrots or sticks."

To the majority in Singapore, however, the new prosperity outweighs the less agreeable aspects of island life. Indeed, it is a tribute to successive (PAP) governments that the principal grievances today are about competitive education, puritanical regulations, over-regimentation and intrusion into private life, whereas formerly they were about food and shelter, social injustice and crime. Moreover, social controls which seem oppressive to the Western world may well be appropriate in the unique circumstances of Singapore. In all his years as prime minister, Lee Kuan Yew never forgot the vulnerability of his tiny, almost resourceless island state. He extolled the necessity for discipline, the need to climb ever higher up the economic ladder. Otherwise, "You will not drop down on a soft paddy field. It is hard, hard concrete. Your bones are broken, and it's *kaput*."

Neon-striped escalators and Chinese lanterns decorate a spacious air-conditioned shopping complex. Such emporiums are magnets for the three million tourists who visit Singapore each year, mainly from Australia, Japan and Britain, and neighbouring countries of South-East Asia.

A doleful eye weeps expressively down a foglamp on a Manila "jeepney". Lovingly decorated, these trucks are the capital's principal mode of public transport. They are the successors of old U.S. Army jeeps which were converted by the Filipinos into minibuses at the end of World War II.

THE VOLATILE PHILIPPINES

To the Spaniards, who ruled over the Philippines from the 16th to the 19th century, the islands were not really a part of the Orient; Spain saw them, rather, as the westernmost point on the map, the farthest outpost of the great Spanish Empire in the Americas. The Imperial picture became an enduring truth. Although the Filipinos live not far from the Asian landmass, descend from Malay and Chinese stock and belong to ASEAN, they are set apart from other Asians by their three centuries of Spanish rule and nearly 50 years under the United States. Filipino society hovers between East and West.

Other peoples in the region were also colonized, of course, but not so early or so thoroughly. In the Philippines, European rule was imposed before any centralized native state had emerged. The Philippines never had a chance to generate a Malacca or a Majapahit. They had developed no traditions of statecraft, no courtly culture; most of the natives had learnt no religion other than the nature worship practised by their far-off ancestors. They were very susceptible to new influences, and they found themselves governed in turn by two powers determined not merely to exploit the territory but to shape its people.

The uniqueness of the Philippines is less apparent today than it was 50 years ago, largely because every other Asian nation has now felt the impact of Western culture. But some striking dif-ferences still separate the Philippines from their neighbours. Notable among them are an emphasis on education and the prevalence of English—both heritages of the American era. In the Philippines, a quarter of those aged between 20 and 24 are at university or college. Literacy is, at 87 per cent, as high as Singapore's and higher than that of most Asian countries. The archipelago has 77 native languages, of which one, Tagalog, is the basis of the official national language, Pilipino. But English is taught in schools as the universal second language, and everybody speaks at least a smattering.

Another peculiarity of the Filipinos is their religion: they are the only predominantly Christian nation in Asia. The Spaniards converted most of them to Catholicism 400 years ago; in this century, American missionaries spread the Protestant faith among the remote tribal peoples. Today 85 per cent of the population are Catholics, 4 per cent worship in the schismatic Philippine Independent Church, which observes Catholic rites, and another 4 per cent are Protestant.

Almost every town of standing in the islands is dominated by a florid baroque church. Parish churches are the hub of community life, and priests and bishops command great authority. The great folk festivals, often attended by hundreds of thousands of participants, are as crowded and colourful as those of Indonesia or India, but the

images that are carried in procession are those of Spanish saints which would not be out of place during Holy Week in Seville.

Enthusiasm is the hallmark of Filipino Catholicism. The faithful crowd the churches to pray before garish portraits of saints and light candles in profusion to their heavenly protectors. On Good Friday, *penitentes* actually have themselves bound to crosses, their hands sometimes even pierced with nails, to act out Christ's passion.

The Spaniards not only gave most Filipinos their religion; they also moulded the very structure of society. They created a feudal hierarchy, totally alien to the co-operative traditions of South-East Asia, which has never been entirely swept away. As a result, abject need—a rarity even in poor countries elsewhere in the region—is widespread at the bottom of Filipino society. Those at the other end of the scale possess extraordinary wealth, power and scope for corruption.

Not surprisingly, Philippine politics have long been troubled and unstable. Most Filipinos take an intense interest in public affairs—to the point of insurrection if the path of democratic opposition is blocked. In this, too, they show themselves different from the South-East Asian norm. In neighbouring countries, dissent may be glossed over in an attempt to reach a workable consensus. In the polarized society of the Philippines, dissent will always come to the fore.

Discord is not a modern phenomenon in these tropical islands. According to myth, it engendered the very land itself. A creation legend describes how the islands of the archipelago were churned up from the ocean floor in the course of an argument between the sea and the sky—a dispute fomented by a mythical bird that was looking for a place to roost.

Many of the 7,107 islands that make up the nation are, in fact, little more than bird rookeries: only about a thousand are inhabited. The total land area is 300,000 square kilometres, of which 11 islands constitute 94 per cent. The most important are Luzon in the north, Mindanao in the south and, between

them, the Visayas group which includes Cebu, Palawan, Samar, Negros, Leyte, Panay and Bohol. Although the Philippines are comparable in area to Italy or the British Isles, their aggregate coastline is nearly as long as that of the United States.

They are among the most spectacularly beautiful islands in the world—not least because most of them are clustered within sight of others, so that almost every palm-fringed coast affords a view across an azure sea to another island lying in the distance. The shallow waters between are a rich source of fish, and much of the Philippines' protein comes from the sea. Most of the larger islands have rugged interior uplands that rise to between 1,000 and 3,000 metres.

Some of the more remote mountain regions are still inhabited by descendants of the earliest human beings to settle in the islands—the people known as Negritos. Most Filipinos, however, are descended from later waves of migrants who introduced a mongoloid stock to the islands—the peoples known as proto-Malays, also from the Asian mainland, and a subsequent group of Malay settlers who probably came by way of Indonesia. By about 300 A.D. the last groups of Malay immigrants were well established in the coastal regions of the Philippines.

The ethnic mixture was further enriched by a steady inflow of other newcomers, especially Chinese who came for trade or plunder and then became enamoured of the islands' beautiful women. Muslim seafarers crossed over from northern Borneo in the late 15th century and brought Islam to Palawan and Mindanao—where the religion of Muhammad flourishes to this day. Within a century, Islam was gaining converts among the local rulers—known as *datus*—in settlements as far north as Luzon.

Before Islam could take a firm hold in the northern islands, the Europeans arrived. In the early 16th century, Ferdinand Magellan landed in the course of his epic bid to circumnavigate the world. Magellan and some of his lieutenants were murdered by Filipinos, but the surviving men, led by Juan Sebastián del Cano, achieved the expedition's goal, making their way back to Europe via the Moluccas and the Cape of Good Hope.

Magellan had hoped to prove, on behalf of Charles I of Spain, that the Spice Islands lay in that part of the world which Pope Alexander VI had assigned to Spain when he divided up the still-unmapped continents between Spain and Portugal. For a while, Magellan's discovery remained a bone of contention between the two rival empires. The issue was not finally resolved in favour of Spain until after the accession of Philip II, in whose honour the islands were renamed the *Islas Filipinas*.

In 1564, the Spanish conquistador Miguel López de Legazpi sailed with 400 men from Mexico to the Philippines. They arrived the following year and founded the first Spanish colony at what is now Cebu City. Later, Legazpi established a fortified settlement on Luzon at Manila, whose magnificent harbour made it the natural focal point of the islands. Legazpi extended Spanish rule by persuading many of the local chieftains to pledge their allegiance in return for retaining their regional power as *datus*.

The Philippines turned out to have no spices worth exporting, but the five Augustinian friars who accompanied Legazpi found them a fertile field for saving souls. For the next three centuries, Spanish friars were to play a decisive role in the unfolding social and economic life of the islands. Not only the Augustinians but other monastic orders—notably the Dominicans, Franciscans and Jesuits—established

5

missing throughout the archipelago, learnt to speak the native languages, introduced new crops such as maize and cocoa from America and taught the "civilized" tribes more efficient and productive farming methods.

Until then, most Filipinos were shifting cultivators who held land in common. The Spanish established a feudal system on the European model, and the hereditary chieftains or *datus* took advantage of the Western concept of private ownership to claim much of the land for themselves. A chasm grew between the local chiefs and the landless peasants, who now had only their new religion to console them. Except for the reclusive high-mountain tribes and the Muslims of the south, whom the Spanish never succeeded in subduing or converting, all Filipinos were eventually received into the Catholic Church—though they still clung to animist modes of thought. Notable among these was the concept of a bargain struck with God: the Filipinos continued to believe that if they made some sacrifice, they were then able to ask for a specific favour to be granted.

Since most of the secular Spanish colonists congregated in Manila—in more than 1,200 villages there was no other Spaniard beside the priest—it was the friars who came to embody the Spanish presence elsewhere in the archipelago. For the most part they exercised a kind of benevolent despotism over the Filipinos, whom by force of Latin-American habit they called *indios*. The colonial government could hardly have functioned without the friars to maintain order among the *indios* and to report back to Manila on what was happening in the provinces. It acknowledged this dependence by putting the priests on its payroll: they became salaried government officials. In time, religious orders and individual bishops were granted great landholdings and became vastly wealthy.

The colonial government, modelled on that of Spanish America, functioned as a subcolony of the Spanish Empire in Mexico rather than as a direct dependency of metropolitan Spain. In theory, the Governor General, who was appointed by the king, held almost unlimited powers. Yet he could govern

effectively only with the help of the friars, and with a military and civil bureaucracy staffed mainly with careerists from Mexico, Peru and Central America, who came to the Philippines to make their fortune. The tradition of using public office for private graft and family profit became ingrained; indeed, it persists to this day at all levels of government.

Economically, the Philippines were almost wholly dependent on Mexico. Cargoes originating in Manila did not go to Spain by the shortest route, round the Cape of Good Hope: by royal decree, designed to prevent Asian goods from competing directly with Spanish products, the Philippines could export only to Mexico. Moreover, Spain also tried, with considerable success, to limit trade to two government-owned ships—called the "Manila Galleons"—which carried East Asian manufactures, mainly Chinese silks, from Manila to Acapulco once or twice a year, and returned laden with silver bullion and minted coin. The profits from this monopoly sustained the Spanish community in Manila and the Chinese merchants who supplied the silks, but did nothing to stimulate local industries.

As Spanish maritime power waned during the 17th and 18th centuries, so did the port's commercial importance. In the early 19th century the Mexican War of Independence finally forced the Spanish government to regard the Philippines as lying in the East rather than in the West, and to take a more active interest in the colony's affairs. Free trade replaced the old monopoly system in 1834. In the wake of increased immigration from Spain, secular culture began to make its appearance in

A Christ-child in Spanish religious dress is borne aloft during a festival in Malolos, 150 kilometres north of Manila. The infant Jesus has been revered in the Philippines since 1521, when his image moved the pagan Queen of Cebu to cry out for baptism.

A CHRONOLOGY OF KEY EVENTS

c. 3000 B.C. Malay peoples start to settle in the islands and form isolated communities.

c. 1400 A.D. The people of the southern islands convert to Islam.

1521 Ferdinand Magellan claims the islands for Spain, but is killed in a skirmish with natives.

1565 Spaniards conquer and begin settling lowland areas of the islands, which they name after their king, Philip II. They subsequently create vast estates for themselves and convert the natives (*below*) to Catholicism.

1572–1811 The Spanish population of Manila derives great wealth from galleons that sail to Acapulco, carrying oriental luxuries on outward journeys and Mexican silver on their return.

1821 Mexico becomes independent; the loss of this rich colony leads Spain to focus more attention on the Philippines. Sugar, tobacco, indigo and hemp are introduced as cash crops.

1896 The Spaniards execute José Rizal, a moderate Filipino campaigner for reform, who becomes a national hero.

1896–1897 An armed revolt against Spanish rule ends in truce and the promise of reforms by the Spaniards.

1898 War breaks out between Spain and the United States (*above, right*). Confident of American support, Filipino rebel leaders declare Independence. American troops force the Spaniards to capitulate but, instead of backing Filipino Independence, the United States takes over the islands.

1907 The U.S. establishes an elected legislative assembly—the first in South-East Asia.

1934 A commonwealth is established, with a Constitution drawn up by Filipinos, and independence is promised after 10 years.

1941–1945 The Japanese occupy the Philippines.

1946 The United States grants independence. It obtains a long lease on a number of Philippine army, navy and air bases.

1965 Ferdinand Marcos (*above*) is elected president.

1969 Communist guerrillas begin a campaign of insurgency which escalates over the years.

1972 Marcos declares martial law in the midst of severe economic and political troubles. It is lifted in 1981.

1986 Marcos is toppled by an army revolt with strong popular support. Corazón Aquino becomes president.

the islands: between 1840 and 1872, 30 newspapers were founded.

Around this time—earlier than in Indonesia or Malaysia—the Philippines saw the emergence of an educated native-born élite. It was made up largely of *mestizos*—a Spanish word that means "of mixed blood", though it bears little of the pejorative sense of the English term "half-caste". By mid-century about a quarter of a million Filipinos were descended from Chinese merchant fathers and *india* mothers: they lived in their own suburb of Manila, Binondo, and dominated many different aspects of trade and agriculture. Another influential *mestizo* community—about 20,000 strong—traced its descent to Spanish or Spanish-American forebears.

Mestizo landowners played a leading role in developing sugar and indigo as export crops, and became major rice producers by leasing land from the friars and subletting it to local sharecroppers. Some of the newly affluent *mestizos* began to travel widely; a number went to Spain for their education. *Mestizo* intellectuals campaigned for political reforms and the abolition of the "friarocracy". The conservative Catholic establishment did its best to maintain the status quo: until 1898 the Church-run University of Santo Tomás in Manila taught essentially the same curriculum that it had in 1611, when it was founded by the Dominicans. The brilliant spokesman for change, the Chinese-*mestizo* physician and scientist José Rizal, had earned doctorates in both Spain and Germany. He wrote two novels dealing with the abuses of Spanish rule in the islands—*Noli Me Tangere* in 1886 and *El Filibusterismo* in 1891—which were both banned by the authorities but

out of food and ammunition supplies.

MacArthur had been ordered to Australia—promising, however, to return—by the time the general in command at Bataan surrendered on April 9, 1942. At the time of the capitulation, the defenders of Bataan numbered some 64,000 Filipinos as well as 12,000 Americans. At least one tenth of them subsequently died of starvation and disease, or were brutally murdered by their Japanese captors, on a gruelling 100-kilometre forced trek to prison camp which later became known as the Death March.

A remnant of the army held out on Corregidor for another month before succumbing to heavy bombardment. The surrender of that force on May 6 officially marked the end of hostilities in the Philippines. Thousands of soldiers from units stationed elsewhere on the islands refused, however, to give themselves up; they simply melted into the mountains and formed themselves into the nuclei of guerrilla organizations. One of the most important was the Communist-led *Hukbalahap*—or Huks, for short.

Just before the fall of Corregidor, Quezon left for America and set up a government in exile. Most of the remaining members of the Filipino élite collaborated with the Japanese who, anxious to enlist support in their military aims, declared the Philippines independent in 1943 and set up a puppet government under José Laurel. The country's new rulers ruthlessly stamped out any subversion, repressed religion and requisitioned rice. From the start of the Japanese domination the mass of the people looked eagerly for an American deliverance. Coast-watchers risked their lives to supply the Allies with vital intelligence about Japanese shipping movements. More than a quarter of a million Filipinos eventually joined the guerrilla groups, which harassed the Japanese army of occupation so effectively that by 1944 the Japanese had control of only 12 of the archipelago's 48 provinces.

In October of that year, MacArthur fulfilled his pledge and returned to the islands, landing on Leyte with four American divisions. Eleven months of bitter fighting followed before Japan surrendered. In all, an estimated one million Filipinos lost their lives during the war, a large proportion of them in the last months of combat; and the final battle for Manila left the capital one of the most extensively war-damaged cities in the world.

Although the Japanese-sponsored regime had been nominally a republic, true independence did not arrive until

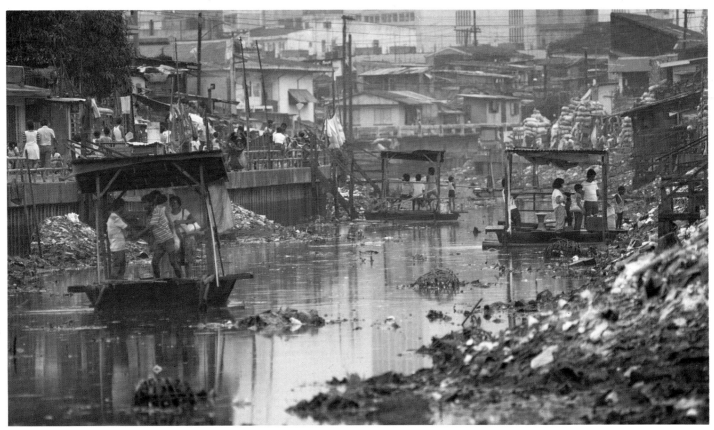

5

July 4, 1946, when Manuel Roxas was sworn in as the first president. The willingness with which the U.S. agreed to surrender its remaining powers left it on cordial terms with its former colony. One consequence was that the U.S. was able to use the Philippines as the centre for its military activities in the western Pacific. It was granted a long lease on Clark Air Base and Subic Bay Naval Base, two huge installations which it had founded in the early years of the century.

The Americans bequeathed to the Philippines a Constitution modelled on their own, with a president and a bicameral congress. During the first 20 years of independence, two parties—the Liberals and the Nationalists—alternated in power. Although the pattern superficially resembled that of United States politics, the reality was rather different. The parties' policies were almost indistinguishable, and politicians readily shifted allegiance from one to the other if it seemed to their advantage. Those in power automatically used their office to enrich themselves. However, elections were held regularly and the succession of new faces at the top gave perennial grounds for hope.

The economic news also fostered optimism. At Independence, the country was overwhelmingly agricultural, growing rice and maize as staples and coconuts and sugar cane for export. But during the 1940s and 1950s, the economy began to diversify. Factories making textiles, shoes and cement appeared. Mining grew in importance. Gold had been extracted from Luzon since the 1930s, but copper production surpassed it in the early 1960s. And the tropical rainforests in the highlands started to yield valuable quantities

of mahogany and other hardwoods.

For the first eight years of independence, trade between the Philippines and the United States remained free, as in the colonial era; from 1954, both countries began to raise tariffs, but it was not until 1974 that Philippine products had to compete on equal terms with other foreign goods in American markets.

The long period of preferential treatment helped the Philippines to grow at an average annual rate of 5 to 6 per cent in the 1950s and 1960s—faster than many of its neighbours. But this success tempted the governments of the time to avoid facing the country's grave underlying problems—an inequitable distribution of land, a burgeoning population and increasing violence in the cities.

The land issue came to a head soon after Independence. About 60 per cent of peasants owned their own plots, most of them small; the rest were tenants, sharecroppers or paid plantation workers subsisting in miserable conditions. The wartime Huk guerrillas took up arms again in the name of peasants' rights and land reform. After years of sporadic fighting in Luzon, Ramon Magsaysay, a former non-Huk guerrilla who became defence secretary in 1950, succeeded in defeating the insurgents militarily. When he became president in 1953, he took a leaf out of the Huks' book and resettled thousands of landless peasant families from Luzon in uncrowded parts of Mindanao and Palawan. Magsaysay wanted to alter land distribution more drastically by limiting the size of holdings and selling the excess from large estates to tenants. But entrenched interests opposed him, and when he was killed in an aeroplane crash in 1957 his more ambitious plans

A mountainside carved by hand
into a stairway of rice terraces
testifies to the labours of Ifugao
tribespeople from northern Luzon.
With their water-retaining dykes,
the terraces have been lovingly
maintained for hundreds— perhaps
even thousands—of years.

5

for land reform remained unrealized.

Meanwhile, population pressures were aggravating the hardships of the poor. The census of 1903 counted 7.6 million Filipinos; 60 years later, the population had risen to about 28 million and was growing at one of the fastest rates in the world—3 per cent per annum. The explosion was largely the result of the introduction of modern public health facilities at the turn of the century. Its effects were all the more serious because of the islands' rugged topography, which crowded people into the fertile valleys. But no government campaign attempted to reduce the birth rate in the Philippines; politicians were not prepared to take on the Catholic Church, which was opposed to birth control.

Violence was in part a heritage from the American era; firearms had been available with few restrictions, as in the United States, and many people had acquired a gun. Landlords had taken to employing armed gangs to bully rebellious tenants. After the Americans left, street crime became a marked problem and lawlessness escalated during the 1950s and 1960s.

In 1965, the Philippines elected a new president on the strength of his supposed ability to remedy such chronic problems as hunger, street crime and government corruption. Ferdinand Marcos, a wartime guerrilla fighter and a noted trial lawyer, earned a great deal of praise during his early years in office for building irrigation systems and introducing improvements in public health, transport and communications. He even achieved a limited measure of land reform in central and northern Luzon. He subsequently contrived to entrench himself in power, to become the most durable and problematical—and in many quarters, the most heartily detested—politician in Philippine history.

In 1969, he became the first president to win a second term of office. The Constitution then in force limited the president to two four-year terms, but outbreaks of violence and civil unrest

during the early 1970s gave him a pretext for declaring martial law in 1972 and forcing through a "reform" Constitution that allowed him to stay on indefinitely as head of state. He kept martial law in force until 1981, ruling by decree though buttressed by a series of referenda on specific points of policy. When his opponents, led by Senator Benigno Aquino, accused him of wanting to establish a "garrison state", Marcos proved them right by imprisoning hundreds, and ultimately thousands, of dissidents. Aquino himself was held in detention for eight years—until May 1980, when he was permitted to travel to the United States for open-heart surgery. In place of the Philippines' accustomed pluralism in party politics, the press and the labour unions, the country was now controlled from the centre, with the army and the security services as Marcos' main instruments of power.

Meanwhile, the seeds of economic crisis were being sown. Marcos' ambitious development projects had been financed by large loans, which in the late 1960s and early 1970s were quite cheap to service. But after the shock to the economies of the Western world caused by the dramatic rise of oil prices in 1973, interest rates soared and the foreign debt of the Philippines increased cripplingly. And to make matters even worse, a slump in world prices for all major Philippine commodities—sugar and coconuts, copper and timber—also drastically reduced the country's foreign earnings.

Many industries were by this time in the hands of associates of Marcos, and being run extremely badly with the sole aim of enriching their owners. When they began to fail in the early 1980s, the government bailed them out, squandering huge sums of money. In the meantime, Marcos himself was abusing the Philippine economy on a scale only conjectured at the time. Through corrupt deals, he amassed a private fortune equivalent to one third of the national debt.

After martial law was lifted in 1981, Marcos was re-elected as head of state. The vote for Marcos was no sure guide to the feelings of the Filipinos since the opposition, convinced that Marcos would rig the results, had boycotted the election. But the turning point in many Filipinos' attitudes came when Benigno Aquino returned from America on August 21, 1983. He was shot dead at Manila Airport as he left the aeroplane. According to the government, the assassin was a Communist agent, Rolando Galman, who was gunned down by soldiers on the spot. The political opposition claimed, however, that the government and the military were involved in Aquino's murder. A civilian fact-finding board concluded that the crime had been planned and executed by a group of conspirators that included many of the country's highest-ranking military officers. The Chief of Staff, General Ver, and 25 other military personnel were eventually put on trial for the shooting but were acquitted.

In the weeks after Aquino's murder, nervous foreign banks withdrew their funds. The Philippines found itself massively in debt to the International Monetary Fund. At first the government refused to comply with the IMF's tough stipulations that public spending and the supply of money be cut drastically. As a result of the government's mishandling of the economy, inflation topped 60 per cent in 1984. When the Filipinos finally swallowed their bitter medicine, inflation came down sharply but most sectors of the economy sank into deep recession. In striking contrast with the burgeoning growth in most other Far Eastern countries, the economy of the Philippines shrank by 5 per cent in 1984, and by another 5 per cent in 1985.

At the worst moments of the slump, one of the few saving graces in the economy was the generosity of Filipinos away from home. More than half a million expatriates work overseas. There are many in the Middle East, labouring on huge construction projects, and another large population in the United States, working at jobs that range from waiter or hotel porter to doctor and university professor. In many other countries, too, Filipinos' literacy and familiarity with Western ways open doors. In 1984, their remittances home were equivalent to 13 per cent of Philippine export income.

The other bright spots in the economy were within the agricultural sector. The introduction of high-yielding rice strains and hybrid maize was transforming productivity. The heavy dependence on sugar and coconuts for export earnings was being progressively lessened by new ventures in coffee, rubber and fish farming.

But the cheerful morsels of economic news were overshadowed by the strains of recession and weariness at President Marcos' long reign. Law and order began to collapse in many areas of the Philippines. Ordinary citizens in the 1980s increasingly found themselves caught in the crossfire between armed groups of the left and right—among them, private armies recruited by corporations or industrialists, miscellaneous bands of robbers and hired killers, as well as various factions

On Negros, steam and reeking smoke belch from the chimneys of the Victorias Milling Company, one of the largest sugar refineries in the world. The island's economy has been devoted almost entirely to sugar production since the 19th century.

113

5

within the army and the police force.

Amid this confusion the Communist movement grew in strength. The Communist Party of the Philippines (CPP) and its military wing, the New People's Army, were established in 1969 after a breakaway from the Soviet-backed Partido Komunista ng Pilipinas. Originally the CPP relied on modest Chinese aid. The funds ceased in 1975 but the CPP, by this time a powerful endogenous force, went from strength to strength. By the mid-1980s, the New People's Army had well over 15,000 guerrilla fighters and was operating in the majority of the country's 73 provinces, mainly in the countryside but also in some cities such as Davao in Mindanao. Where they deemed it necessary, the Communists used ruthless techniques to gain the ascendancy. They would shoot local mayors and heads of villages to terrorize the people and weaken the local administration.

One of the few moderating influences on the political scene was the Catholic Church. Cardinal Jaime Sin, the Archbishop of Manila, offered constructive criticism of the Marcos regime, although not to the point of encouraging the extreme left. The Church was split between those behind Marcos and the majority who followed the Cardinal's middle way. There was also a handful, perhaps 1 per cent, who supported the Communists and even worked with them.

Political passions in the Philippines were already running high when canvassing began for the 1986 presidential elections. In the course of a campaign marred by bloodshed and murder, Marcos' supporters subjected the electoral process to every kind of abuse from vote-buying to the theft of ballot boxes. Eventually Marcos proclaimed himself the winner, with 53 per cent of the vote. The opposition, led by the widow of the murdered Benigno Aquino, contested the result with massive, non-violent demonstrations.

Two weeks after the election charade, a group of army officers, led by the defence minister Juan Ponce Enrile, proclaimed open revolt against the Marcos regime. Thousands of Manila's citizens thronged the road to the rebels' camp and prevented government troops from reaching it. As Marcos' position became untenable, Mrs. Corazón Aquino was sworn in as the Philippines' new president. Twelve hours later Marcos was persuaded to leave the country. No sooner had he gone than Mrs. Aquino opened his opulent Manila palace to the public so that ordinary Filipinos could judge the outrageously extravagant lifestyle of the autocrat who had ruled them for 21 years. They came by the thousand to gape at the lofty rooms and old master paintings—not to mention Mrs. Marcos' gold washbasin and 2,700 pairs of shoes.

Mrs. Aquino drew support from all over the Philippines, but nowhere was the commitment stronger than in Manila, where every class from the business élite to the poorest of the poor had glimpsed the excesses of their former leader and his family. It was the people of Manila who were at the centre of the struggle to oust Marcos, and they who rejoiced most ecstatically at the change of rule.

Manila habitually sets the course for the rest of the country. It is not only the hub of Filipino politics but also the centre of the country's economy, religion, entertainment and communications. It is the home of two thirds of the Philippines' industries, and its harbour is the scene of a constant coming and going of cargo vessels from ports all over the world. Every year Manila draws hundreds of thousands of newcomers, who add to its already immense population and its burden of social problems. In 1903, Manila had a population of 220,000; modern Metro Manila, the term used to describe the conurbation which now links 13 suburban cities and towns with the Manila of old, has seven million inhabitants and is still growing fast. Its centre is full of reminders of the past—old Spanish forts, a Christian churchyard guarded by Chinese lions—yet the present intrudes everywhere. Like all great Asian cities, Manila is intensely dynamic, noisy, overcrowded, snarled in endless traffic jams, whose most eye-catching constituents are jeepneys—gaudily decorated trucks converted into bus-cum-taxis, that have become the unofficial emblem of the place.

Metro Manila has more than 100 cinemas, and there is a thriving and sometimes innovative Philippine film industry. Another of Manila's addictions is the Basque sport of *jai alai*, one of the heritages of Spanish rule. The action is something like squash except that players wield crescent-shaped wicker baskets instead of rackets. Spectators place bets on the outcome of this fastest of all ball games.

For people with money to spend, there are avenues lined with restaurants famous for some of the finest cooking in the East, and nightclubs where Filipino jazzmen uphold their reputation as the best musicians in Asia. There is also a variety of pleasure dens and massage "clinics" where one can form relationships that, as one guidebook delicately phrases it, are "intensified by their briefness and generally monetary nature".

Not far from the glamorous boulevards of affluent Manila lies a very different world—the twisted alleys of Tondo, where around 250,000 squatters live jammed together in tin-roofed shanties. With virtually no plumbing, the stench is appalling, but television aerials rise high above many of the ramshackle dwellings to proclaim to the world that things are looking up. Many people manage to live an honest and quasi-normal life in these squalid surroundings, perhaps picking rags and scrap metal from the city's rubbish dumps, but many resort to prostitution and crime. Manila's slums are dangerous places, where outsiders only venture in broadest daylight and in groups of three or more. The litter-strewn alleys make a perfect hideout for fugitives, racketeers and malefactors.

Those who have turned to petty thievery to rise above the anonymous poverty of the slums sometimes move on to grand larceny as a respectable way of life. Manila has long been a violent place and today it has organized gangsterism reminiscent of Chicago in the Al Capone era; there is said to be a murder every hour.

The peasant life the Tondo squatters left behind begins only a short distance from the outskirts of the capital. Villages are mostly unplanned agglomerations of one and two-storey frame houses, some with corrugated-iron roofs and others with palm thatch. A good part of everyday life is lived in perpetually green gardens wreathed with vines and flowers, or on a sandy patch by the sea.

If the village is large enough to warrant a town hall, a school or a hospital, it may also have a public park adorned

with a statue of the scholarly revolutionary José Rizal, bending over his writing table with a kerosene lamp at his side. Nearby there will be the restaurants and cafés where people spend their free time sitting under awnings, sipping soft drinks and talking volubly: Filipinos have a lot to say to each other, even if they have been neighbours for 20 years. If there is a bus stop nearby, each bus will be greeted by girls offering bananas or oranges or home-made sweets to passengers through the open windows; competition is fierce but good-natured.

For most rural families, the income from such commerce is a sideline to farming or fishing. On many of the smaller islands, where space is scarce, the land is divided into peasant small-holdings, each growing a variety of crops. The bulk of the Philippines' rice comes from the largest island, Luzon, whose extensive central lowlands permit large-scale agriculture.

Most of the sugar plantations in the Philippines are concentrated in the fourth largest island, Negros. Until the 19th century, Negros was almost un-inhabited, but by 1893 it harboured 274 steam-operated sugar mills, with hundreds of thousands of acres of sugar-cane fields to supply them and a vast population of agricultural workers who had immigrated from nearby islands. For decades the sugar industry gave a livelihood directly or indirectly to about 5 million people, but the decline in world sugar prices in the 1980s bankrupted many plantations. Few of the unemployed field hands have found alternative work; they face the choice between the squalor of a city slum and a life of desperate poverty in the lush green countryside. Eventually, some may be rescued by tourism,

5

for Negros, seen from afar, is a Hollywood stereotype of an island paradise. Its purple mountains are capped with white clouds and descend to superb beaches and underwater gardens of coral reefs; hot springs and waterfalls abound in its forests.

Some Philippine islands have already adapted themselves to the tourist economy. In parts of Cebu and Panay, for example, villages of *nipah* huts—a palm thatch and bamboo version of a motel cabin—have sprung up to accommodate the Swiss, Australians and Californians who represent the forward edge of the tourist invasion. Hotels and beach clubs follow hard on the heels of the huts, and in places only the old folk are left working the land, while all the young people are busy as waiters, massage girls or peddlers of coral necklaces.

Still, there are communities in the Philippines that have not yet succumbed to the blandishments of modernism. The 1.5 million Muslims of western Mindanao, Palawan and the Sulu archipelago constitute a prime example of a fiercely independent people still clinging to the traditions they inherited from their ancestors. Other Filipinos call them the *moros*. The word is a misnomer, bestowed by the early Spanish colonizers, who had just finished driving the Moors from Spain, and to whom all Muslims were *moros*. Ethnically the Philippine Muslims are scarcely less Malay than the rest of the islands' population, though their aquiline noses suggest an admixture of Arab stock. Ideologically, however, they are a race apart. They have never been reconciled to any central government, and in the 1970s they began a simmering guerrilla war against the republic's authority. In 1976, the government agreed in principle to grant the Moros considerable regional autonomy, including their own judiciary, legislature and security force. So far, however, little of substance has been devolved.

The Moros wear the most striking costumes of the Philippines—the men,

sarongs with braided waistcoats and wide cummerbunds, topped with a fez or a turban; many are armed with a more than merely decorative dagger. The women wear trousers with sari-like robes or brocade jackets whose golden threads and shining buttons sparkle in the sun.

The Moros live in hierarchic communities under sultans and *datus* who also administer the religious courts known as *agama*. They practise polygamy, which is technically illegal but is tolerated by the government, and observe the Koranic law by which a man can repudiate a wife whenever he wishes. Yet women are much freer to come and go as they please than women in most other Islamic societies, and the literacy rate is as high among Moro women as among Moro men.

The Muslim coastal tribes—Samal, Yakan and Tausug—make their living from the sea, mainly as fishermen but also as inter-island traders, and occasionally as smugglers and pirates. The southernmost islands of the Sulu archipelago are considered bandit country and no-go areas for outsiders without the proper introductions. The Samal travel for hundreds of kilometres in home-made boats that are often only hollowed-out logs buoyed by twin outriggers, fitted with a single sail. During World War II, an outrigger manned by escaping Samals and Americans made the 5,000-kilometre crossing to Australia under sail.

The Filipinos with the closest ties to the sea, however, are the Bajau Laut— a group of no more than 20,000 to 30,000 people, many of whom spend all of their lives on small houseboats. The whole of their sea-gypsy life is governed by the tides. When typhoons lash the islands, they will ride out the storm aboard their boats rather than try to seek safety on land: terra firma makes them feel "landsick". Children are born, love affairs are consummated and marriages are celebrated aboard the boats. Hardly touched by the modern world, the Bajau Laut rarely know how old they are or what year it is.

Other Filipinos might envy the detachment of the Bajau Laut. Most of the islanders—city-dwellers and country folk alike—have been unable to escape the momentous upheavals that have buffeted their country in recent years. The martial law of the 1970s, the economic crisis of the mid-1980s, Marcos' sudden departure in 1986, generated waves that reached almost every corner. Communist insurgency has represented a far more serious threat to the status quo here than in other ASEAN countries. Elsewhere, Communism has normally been associated with ethnic minorities—such as the Chinese in Malaysia—or has been bolstered from outside. But under Marcos' repressive yoke, Filipino Communism burgeoned as a native movement with growing popular support.

Even if democracy in the post-Marcos era succeeds in quelling extremism, the reconstruction of Filipino society is bound to be a long and painful task. Under 21 years of Marcos' rule, every institution from village headships to the supreme court was filled from the ranks of his cronies. Until the institutions are again representative and viable, the Philippines is unlikely to find the will radically to tackle economic and social problems.

The other members of ASEAN are nervously watching their volatile neighbour. During Marcos' last years in power, the Philippines came to be seen as the odd man out in the group, and the other heads of state avoided Manila. While taking advantage of the economic weakness of the Philippines to expand their own trade, its partners feared contagion with the Communist Insurgency. The more authoritarian among them were disconcerted by the popular movement that swept Corazón Aquino to power. Indonesia and Malaysia, intent on keeping religion out of politics, looked askance at the Church's prominent political role. If the Philippines succeeds in regaining its equilibrium, its neighbours will sigh with relief to find that ASEAN's most serious internal threat to stability has at last been overcome.

Against a backdrop of high-rise hotels lining a waterfront boulevard, pleasure craft are moored in the Manila Yacht Club marina. The building dominating the near shore was built for the 1974 Miss Universe contest; it now serves as a theatre and cultural centre.

AMPHIBIOUS LIVING IN A REMOTE ARCHIPELAGO

Among the denizens of the Sulu archipelago in the southernmost Philippines are many who are more at home on the sea than on land. The Samal, an Islamic race of farmers and seafarers, colonize the shallows round the islands' shores with villages built on stilts. The watery expanses surrounding their homes afford some protection against intruders in an area notorious for lawlessness.

Scattered among the Samal, the autonomous Bajau Laut have taken amphibious existence a stage further; some of them pass their entire lives afloat, roaming the coasts in little houseboats. The boat-dwellers depend for their livelihood on fishing and a modicum of trade with the Samal. For generations these sea-gypsies have been the poorest of the archipelago's peoples; their water-borne homes are picturesque but primitive, providing cramped and uncomfortable living quarters. Traditionally disdained by their neighbours, many Bajau Laut have of recent years taken to stilt-building, seeing a settled home as the key to a better status.

A Bajau Laut family set out on a fishing expedition in the houseboat that is their permanent home. Its roof of wood and plastic scraps shelters five or six square metres of living space in which adults and children alike must eat, work and sleep.

In a stilt village near Zamboanga, a town on the westernmost tip of Mindanao, a Samal man relaxes on his porch. Every day the tides bring fish almost to his door and then flush away household sewage.

A settlement near Sitangkai at the archipelago's southern tip provides shelter and mooring space for a community of Bajau Laut. The houses perch on stilts above a submerged coral reef two kilometres offshore.

At high tide, boats provide the only links between houses in Sitangkai, mainly inhabited by Bajau Laut.

On the porch of her one-room home, a Samal woman kneads washing and her daughter prepares vegetables. A straw mat shelters them from the sun.

Samal women set up a vegetable stall on a meandering bridge that links the land and sea villages of Rio Hondo, near Zamboanga.

In the metal light of dawn, an outrigger glides into Zamboanga harbour with a cargo of helmet shells destined to catch the eye of tourists. Boats such as these, the workhorses of the Samal, can reach speeds of over 20 kilometres per hour when the wind is up.

Smiling figures and miniature craft
mark Bajau Laut graves on the island
of Great Santa Cruz near Zamboanga,
used as a cemetery by the boat-
dwellers. Excluding visits to market,
the Bajau Laut are only brought
ashore by death.

Workmen, balanced on bamboo
scaffolding, restore a gilded roof at
Wat Phra Keo, Thailand's most
magnificent Buddhist temple complex.
The ornate buildings, glittering with
glass mosaic and Chinese ceramics,
stand within the walls of the royal
palace in Bangkok.

AN UNCONQUERED KINGDOM

Geography sets Thailand apart from the other members of ASEAN. Located on the Asian mainland, the country largely escaped the main historic seaborne influences that shaped the maritime world to the south and east—notably the Muslim religion and European rule. But Thailand has been far closer than the other members of ASEAN to the succession of crises that have plagued Indochina in the decades following World War II. Since the invasion of Cambodia in 1979 by Thailand's old rival Vietnam, Thailand has been the only ASEAN state directly confronting an expansionist Communist power across its national border.

Thailand's cultural affinities are overwhelmingly with its mainland neighbours. Like the people of Burma, Cambodia, Laos and parts of southern China, the Thais are Buddhists of the Theravada orthodoxy—the form of the religion closest to the Buddha's teachings. Offering a liberating "middle path" between extremes of reason and passion, asceticism and sensuality, it has shaped the Thais into a people who eschew extremism and fundamentalism. Foreign visitors to Thailand invariably note with delight the grace and decorum of the people, their sense of fun and their concern for the well-being of others. Buddhist lessons of correct action and speech, of non-violence and loving-kindness, have greatly contributed to such traits.

While sharing their Buddhist culture with their neighbours, Thais are acutely aware of a history that they feel makes them unique. There has been a major Thai state in the present territory of Thailand since the 14th century, and the country is one of the very few in Asia to have escaped Western colonialism. The monarchy is a potent symbol of the country's historical continuity and a focus for celebrations of nationhood. In 1982 there was a grandiose commemoration of the 200th anniversary of the founding of Bangkok and the Chakri dynasty, of which King Bhumibol Adulyadej is the ninth monarch in direct succession.

Devotion to the monarchy, to Buddhism and to the idea of the nation creates a distinctive Thai identity which is strengthened by a cultural uniformity more marked than in the other large members of ASEAN. The country has not the multiplicity of languages found in Indonesia and the Philippines, nor such a complex ethnic mixture as Malaysia. Thai is the first language of at least 85 per cent of the population of 50 million, and is understood by almost everyone. Thai is a member of a large cluster of languages, which are spoken in all bordering countries as well as southern China and northern Vietnam. Unlike Malay, they are monosyllabic and tonal.

For all their similarities, the Thais are not quite the single harmonious family that they seem at first glance. They fall into several groups which

A neon sign cryptically advertises a restaurant on one of Bangkok's main streets. The capital offers some of the most varied nightlife in the world, ranging from the refined to the salacious—from folk dramas and musical evenings to bars, discotheques and massage parlours.

The illuminations of the Royal Orchid Sheraton Hotel are reflected in the still surface of Bangkok's Chao Phraya river. With more than two million foreign visitors a year, Thailand's tourist industry ranks alongside rice as the highest foreign exchange earner.

speak different dialects of Thai and have their own traditions of folklore and music. The four main groups— the inhabitants of the central plain, the southerners, the northerners, and the north-easterners—correspond to the main geographical divisions of the country, which only came under centralized rule late in the last century.

Thailand's great central plain was formerly forested but now consists of unbroken paddy fields. It is the most fertile part of the country and it grows the bulk of Thailand's rice. Almost since Thailand first became an independent kingdom, the capital has been located here and the people of the central plain have been the dominant group in the country.

The long neck of land to the south which links central Thailand with Malaysia is somewhat less fertile than the central plain. For the past century, it has been a rubber-growing area. The people of the region have long been ruled by the central Thais and, though their dialect sets them apart, most of them live in the same way.

North and west of the central plain, the land rises to forested mountains. Here, again, rice is grown, together with more temperate crops such as maize. Until the late 19th century, the northern Thais belonged to a semi-independent kingdom which paid tribute to the central Thai kingdom but conducted its own affairs.

The vast north-eastern region, separated from Laos by the meandering Mekong river, is a high plateau cursed with infertile soil and low rainfall. This is the poorest area of Thailand: about seven million people are officially categorized as living in poverty in the north-east. Like the north, this region had a history of semi-autonomy up to

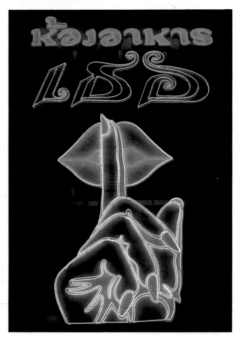

the late 19th century: the people speak the same language as the Lao across the border, and they have at times been linked politically with Lao kingdoms.

In the outlying regions and especially the north-east, many people chafe with a sense of material neglect and of social disparagement by national government. But the central Thai ascendancy plays down regional loyalties and discontents; it requires its own version of the language to be taught in schools throughout the country, and in government publications and school textbooks the unity of the nation is constantly proclaimed.

The concept of unity must accommodate not only the Thai populations but also the 15 per cent who are not Thai. The largest ethnic minority, comprising about 4 million—8 per cent of the total population—are Chinese, many of whom arrived in the late

19th and early 20th centuries. They have long dominated Thai business.

The Chinese in Thailand are assimilated to a far greater degree than in either Islamic Malaysia or Indonesia. Dietary restrictions do not hinder social intercourse: the Thais, unlike Muslim peoples, eat pork. There are no barriers to intermarriage, which has occurred at all social levels in Thailand from the peasantry to the royal family. Moreover the Chinese are happy to embrace Thailand's Buddhism.

The next largest minority consists of people of Malay ancestry who practise the Muslim faith—though they live otherwise in very much the same way as the Thais. They account for about 3 per cent of the population and are largely concentrated in four provinces close to the Malaysian border.

There is a third broad category of peoples of non-Thai origin, numbering considerably fewer than one million, who mainly inhabit the hills and forest areas of the north. They include the Akha, Hmong, Karen, Khmu, Lahu, Lawa, Lisu, Yao and Lao. Some, such as the Lawa, have been in Thailand as long as the Thais, while others have arrived in this century. Most are animists, but some have been converted to Christianity or Buddhism. Most, from necessity, practise shifting rice cultivation; many would become wet-rice farmers like their Thai neighbours if there were suitable land. Until recently, the isolated hill peoples scarcely made any impact on the consciousness of their compatriots. Even now, they are somewhat grudgingly accepted and some have not yet been granted Thai citizenship. Most are very poor.

The one source of money traditionally available to the hill peoples has been opium. The poppies are grown

throughout the Golden Triangle—the notorious stretch of land where Thailand, Burma and Laos meet. Besides producing some of the opium itself, Thailand has been the major conduit to the West for Burmese opium. In the early 1970s, the United States, alarmed at its soaring addiction rates, put pressure on Thailand to suppress the drug. The Thais toughened their legislation against makers and transporters of narcotics and stepped up surveillance. For several years the measures had little effect, mainly because many government officials had a corrupt interest in the trade. In recent years, however, both trafficking and internal production have dropped, and some efforts have been made to find alternative cash crops, such as tea and tobacco, for the hill peoples.

The non-Thais living in Thailand also include some Vietnamese, who settled in the north-east in the 1940s and 1950s to escape the fighting against the French in their own country, and hundreds of thousands of Cambodians, many of whom flooded across the Cambodia-Thai border as refugees after the 1979 Vietnamese invasion of Cambodia. The host country has generally pursued a tolerant and humane attitude towards the refugees, but they remain in camps along the border and are not assimilated into the life of Thailand.

The Thais themselves only arrived in their land during historic times. Speakers of Thai and its related languages probably originated in the southern and south-western parts of what is now China. During the first thousand years A.D. they spread in a southerly direction along river valleys as far as northern Burma and Assam to the south-west and northern Laos and Vietnam to the south-east.

Wherever they stopped, they coexisted for long periods with other ethnic groups. They paid tribute to powerful states such as the Mon kingdoms of Burma and northern Thailand, and the Khmer empire centred in Cambodia. These states were already strongly subject both to Buddhist and to Hindu influences. Eventually the Thais, too, embraced the Buddhist religion and many Hindu customs. They practised irrigated rice cultivation and, where they had some autonomy, they organized themselves into loose federations of small local territories—often single valleys, each controlled by a chief

These federations worked well when the Thais inhabited mountain terrain where communications were difficult. But as they edged southwards into the flatter expanses of Thailand, centra-

6

lized political systems became more practical. By the 13th century, several small Thai states had emerged. A kingdom based at Sukhothai, at the northern end of the central plain, was the earliest; another kingdom, which was centred on Chiang Mai in the north, followed soon after.

The greatest of the early Thai states was the kingdom of Ayutthaya, founded in 1351 as the Khmer empire was waning. It was known as Siam by the Khmer, Europeans and other outsiders. From its eponymous capital on the Thai central plain, Ayutthaya claimed suzerainty over all the territory of present-day Thailand, together with parts of Malaya, Burma, Cambodia,

southern China and Laos. The other Thai kingdoms were to varying degrees vassals of Ayutthaya. In its turn, Ayutthaya paid tribute to the Emperor of China. Ayutthaya was to retain its dominance for more than 400 years.

The Ayutthaya kingdom developed ideas about the exercise of power which resonate to this day in state rituals and the popular imagination. The king both represented and sought to maintain a symbolic harmony of earthly and cosmic forces. At times he was referred to as a future Buddha or, in a more Hindu idiom, as a god-king.

The social and political order was symbolically constructed as a model of the Hindu-Buddhist universe. The

king on his throne was identified with the Hindu god Indra who ruled one of the heavens from the top of Mount Meru, the cosmological centre of the world. The royal capital had three concentric moats and ramparts representing the three seas surrounding Mount Meru. A hierarchy of princes and officials mirrored the retinue of lords serving Indra.

Elaborate trappings emphasized each functionary's place in the hierarchy. The king's person, for example, was on state occasions surmounted by nine tiers of umbrellas, equivalent to the crown of European rulers; the rulers of the tributary states were accorded umbrellas of lesser scale. The

senior officials were given a set of symbolic objects denoting their rank, which included cushions, seals, utensils for preparing betel nut—a mild narcotic—and spittoons for disposing of their betel-stained saliva. And, on appointment, each official was also given a new name.

Nowadays, the nine umbrellas still form part of the king's regalia, and every government employee down to primary school teachers wears a uniform with his grade proclaimed on his shoulder. The display of rank has become ingrained in Thai society.

The Ayutthaya kings devised enduring strategies for maintaining a more than symbolic hold on power. One of them was centralization. Independent local princes were converted wherever possible into court functionaries, and thus detached from their natural constituency of support. There was no separate military: all officials were supposed to raise armies, and manpower was used for civil or military purposes according to need.

Even the Buddhist order of monks was co-opted to provide the State with moral legitimacy and a means of controlling its subjects. Monasteries established throughout the kingdom helped to assert the presence of the State. The monkhood was generally flexible and prepared to accommodate the political order for the sake of securing the adherence of rulers to Buddhist values. Little has changed in these respects. There is still considerable overlap between secular and religious life.

What has changed profoundly is the economic basis of the State. The material power of the Ayutthaya kingdom rested on the conscripted or enslaved labour of the people and on a system of royal trading monopolies. Everyone in the population other than the king, who was above rank, was given a number that indicated both his entitlements and obligations towards his superiors. The highest-ranking individual below the king was the viceroy, with 100,000 points. Other nobles appointed by the king had between 400 and 100,000 points. The great majority of citizens, with 25 points or fewer, laboured either directly for the king or for the small class of officials and aristocrats. At the bottom came beggars and slaves, with five points. The fact that they were designated any points at all indicates that they had some rights, notably recourse to justice.

European contact with the Ayutthaya kingdom began in the 16th century. The Portuguese sent an embassy in 1509 and were soon providing training in musketry and gunnery. The Dutch followed the Portuguese, and in 1609 a Siamese embassy was received at The Hague. In 1612, British traders brought a respectful letter from King James I to the Siamese king and reported back that Ayutthaya was a city as large and impressive as London. For much of the 17th century, Europeans were granted rights to trade with Ayutthaya. But the Siamese, rightly, suspected the Europeans of imperial and missionary ambitions and terminated relations in the late 17th century. Apart from a few isolated visits, links with Europe ceased until well into the 19th century. Ayutthaya remained a cosmopolitan city nonetheless, with a substantial Chinese population, a corps of Japanese guards, and many Turkish, Arabic and Persian traders.

In 1767, a Burmese army defeated the kingdom and sacked and burnt the capital. The Siamese soon rallied after this disaster, ousted the Burmese and re-established their realm. Instead of rebuilding the city, they founded a new capital further south at Thonburi, then moved it to nearby Bangkok in 1782. The territory of the kingdom was expanded and commerce encouraged.

During the reigns of King Mongkut (1851–1868) and his son King Chulalongkorn (1868–1910), change accelerated. Mongkut was the original for the larger-than-life monarch in the Rodgers and Hammerstein musical *The King and I*, which was based on the memoirs of the British governess employed to educate some of the King's 82 children. The show caricatured Mongkut as a capricious Oriental tyrant; in reality, his harem notwithstanding, he was a highly educated and sophisticated man. He and his son Chulalongkorn directed the country on the one hand towards modernization and reform, which were to forestall European empire builders in their search for territory, and on the other hand towards increasing state absolutism.

Forced labour and debt bondage were gradually eliminated; slavery was abolished completely in 1905. The country's infrastructure was developed: thousands of Chinese arrived annually to be employed as wage labour, building canals, ports and—later—railways. Meanwhile, the monarchs strengthened their positions by appointing brothers and other relations as ministers and regional governors in place of the provincial aristocracy. These developments were generally encouraged and supported by Western countries, which began to show a new interest in relations with Siam.

In 1855, Sir John Bowring, British governor of Hong Kong, negotiated a treaty with King Mongkut, who soon signed similar agreements with other

On the outskirts of Mae Hong Son, a village of 6,000 people in northwestern Thailand, a Buddhist temple compound nestles in a forest enclave. Although the temple is the spiritual heart of most Thai communities, it is usually built in a secluded quarter.

6

industrializing countries in Europe. These pacts allowed Westerners valuable economic and legal privileges. The King gave up his monopoly on trade, and importers only had to pay a tax of 3 per cent of their goods' value; imports of opium and bullion were duty free. The British wanted to buy rice to feed the immigrant workers in Malaya, and the Thai people, as they emerged from forced labour and slavery, were encouraged to cultivate new land. King Chulalongkorn invited Westerners to act as ministerial advisers. He sent his sons to be educated in Berlin, London and St. Petersburg.

Thanks in no small part to its rulers' astuteness, Siam remained sovereign over its core territory. But the British and the French were consolidating their positions in South-East Asia, and they coveted many of Siam's outlying regions. The country had to accept considerable losses of territory to colonial Burma, Cambodia, Laos and Malaya. And the British, holding key financial advisory posts, dominated Siam's economy until World War II.

The effort to build a modern Siamese state faltered for a while after the death of King Chulalongkorn in 1910, but King Prajadhipok, who ascended the throne in 1925, was a reformer anxious to share decision-making with his ministers. He even considered giving the country a Constitution, but was resisted by his ministers. Some of his younger, Western-educated officials, however, were less eager to abandon the idea, and thought the time was ripe for such a change. In 1932, a group of civil servants and army officers engineered a bloodless *coup d'état* which swept away the senior ministers and put an end to absolute monarchy. The coup was not directed against the King himself, who was kept on as constitutional head of state.

The new young leaders of Siam were the first generation outside the royal family to be educated abroad and instilled with Western ideas. The civilian element included men of socialist leanings, among them Pridi Phanomyong who was later to become regent. But it was the military which predominated. Nationalism was in the air, and in the prevailing atmosphere the army seemed the natural successor to the absolute monarchy; besides, the army was better equipped and better organized than any other Thai institution.

The military have dominated Thai politics during most of the intervening decades. Early on, they set a pattern of authoritarian rule which is still in evidence to some extent. But Thailand has escaped the extremes suffered under most military regimes. Because the country's rulers have been able to rely on the traditional loyalty and obedience of the people, they have usually achieved the control they desired by using comparatively limited amounts of violence and intimidation.

Nationalist sentiments dominated the first years of constitutional monarchy. Direct state involvement in industrial and commercial enterprises was encouraged, and the Chinese suffered legal discrimination. Siam was renamed Thailand in 1939 in accordance with patriotic enthusiasms of the time. The nationalists were attracted by European and Japanese fascist models; their expansionist rhetoric found expression in a short war against the French in Laos and Cambodia during 1940 and 1941.

At the end of 1941, the Japanese demanded access through Thailand by air, land and sea en route to attack the British in Burma and Malaya. Thailand resisted for less than a day, then opted for self-preservation. The Prime Minister allowed the Japanese forces military rights of passage in return for assurances of respect for national independence. But many Thai leaders, including Pridi and the Washington ambassador, Seni Pramoj, resisted the Japanese ascendancy. When Thailand's ruling regime declared war on Britain and the United States in 1942, Seni Pramoj refused to deliver the

A 19th-century mural depicts a scene from the Ramakien, the Thai version of the Indian Ramayana epic. In this episode, the white monkey-general Hanuman inflates his body into a living bridge to allow the army of the hero Rama to cross a river.

A CHRONOLOGY OF KEY EVENTS

c. 600–900 A.D. Mon people originating in west China form kingdoms in Thailand. Missionaries from Ceylon convert the Mon to Buddhism. Thai people from southern China begin to move southwards. Some settle among the Mon in Thailand and form small states.

c. 900–1300 The Khmer, relations of the Mon, rule an empire based in Cambodia which extends over most of present-day Thailand. The Mon introduce the Khmer and the Thai to Buddhism.

1238 Thai chieftains in the northern part of Thailand's central plain defeat their Khmer overlords and found the first independent Thai kingdom of Sukhothai.

1350–1767 As Sukhothai declines, a new Thai kingdom based at Ayutthaya in the south rises to prominence. In this rich state, architecture, bronze sculpture (*below*) and literature all reach new heights.

1509 The Portuguese send an embassy to Ayutthaya, initiating nearly two centuries of contact with Europe.

1688 General Phra Phetracha, suspecting sinister motives in French missionaries and ambassadors welcomed by the King, stages a *coup d'état* and inaugurates a 150-year period of Thai isolation from the West.

1767–1782 A Burmese army conquers and burns the city of Ayutthaya and decimates its population. The brilliant Thai general, Taksin, drives out the Burmese. Assuming the royal title, he founds a new capital at Thonburi, adjacent to modern Bangkok.

1782–1809 General Chakkri mounts a successful coup and founds the present Thai ruling house. He moves the capital to Bangkok.

1851–1868 The scholar-king, Mongkut (*above*), ends the policy of isolation, signing treaties of friendship and commerce with several Western powers. His country, now known as Siam, quickly becomes a major exporter of rice.

1868–1910 King Chulalongkorn modernizes Siam rapidly. He abolishes slavery, founds schools, encourages study abroad and builds railways and roads.

1932 A military and civilian group leads a bloodless coup against absolute monarchy. The king remains as a constitutional symbol.

1939 Siam is renamed Thailand.

1941–1945 During World War II, Thailand allows access to Japanese troops to invade Burma and Malaya. In 1942, Thailand declares war on Britain and the United States. However, the Free Thai Movement contributes to Allied efforts to resist the Japanese.

1947 The army takes over the government. It rules for most of the next few decades, allowing varying degrees of civilian participation.

1965–1976 Supporting American action in Vietnam, Thailand plays host to large numbers of troops and aircraft.

1973 Student demonstrations bring down the military government, inaugurating three years of civilian democratic rule.

1976 A *coup d'état* reinstates the army in power.

declaration to the U.S. government.

A "Free Thai" anti-Japanese movement was formed in 1944. The war ended before it could make a material contribution to the Allies' cause but its endeavours meant that Thailand was spared the full disadvantages of being a hostile nation. It became one of the first Asian countries to join the United Nations in 1946.

After a brief post-war period of civilian government and a flowering of democratic and trade union freedoms, the military regained its dominant position. The army and the police (who in Thailand are equipped with tanks, aircraft and heavy weapons) were greatly strengthened in the 1950s by American military aid. Thai governments began to ally themselves enthusiastically to the United States and to take up the vehemently anti-Communist position they still maintain. Thai soldiers fought in the Korean War in the 1950s and later saw action in Vietnam. The headquarters of the anti-Communist South-East Asia Treaty Organization (SEATO) was first established in Bangkok in 1954.

Senior military and police were not only interested in politics and warfare. They also established themselves on the boards of innumerable financial and commercial companies and grew rich through illegal and corrupt economic practices. One notorious police chief, General Phao, made his fortune in the opium trade; the future prime minister, General Sarit Thanarat, became wealthy by diverting funds from the Lottery Bureau.

Sarit seized power by a bloodless *coup d'état* in 1957. Despite his personal venality, his six-year period of power laid the groundwork for much of the economic growth that has since

6

Miniature shrines shelter the guardian
deities of homes and businesses in
Thai cities and countryside alike. Set
on pillars in gardens or on rooftops,
the spirit houses range from what look
like wooden dovecotes *(right)* to
elaborate and expensive replicas of
temples *(left and centre)*.

occurred in Thailand, keeping its per capita income well ahead of that of Indonesia though not as high as Malaysia's. At the World Bank's urging, new policies were introduced in Thailand's first Five Year National Development Plan, launched in 1961. Direct state involvement in the economy decreased; and private and foreign investment were promoted. The government spent heavily on infrastructure such as roads and electric power, urban development and education. The boom continued after Sarit's death, to provide an average 8.6 per cent growth rate for the 1960s, nearly double that of the previous decade.

The fastest expansion was seen in the manufacturing, service and mining sectors. Thailand is estimated to have 12 per cent of the world's reserves of tin,

and tin production made a sizeable contribution to export earnings. From the early 1970s Thailand has been the world's largest producer of rubies and sapphires. Manufacturing centred at first on basic import substitution such as cement, and on consumer goods for the home market such as textiles, beer and soft drinks. Much wealth became concentrated in a few large conglomerates controlling many companies, but small family firms employing up to 10 people were—and remain—a feature of the Thai economy.

Agriculture declined in importance relative to manufacturing; its contribution to the national economy was to shrink from more than 50 per cent in the late 1950s to less than 20 per cent in the 1980s. Agricultural production was still expanding however. Despite

a fast-growing population, Thailand's peasant farmers continued to produce enough rice to feed their compatriots and leave a surplus for export. Today, Thailand is the world's fifth largest producer of rice and the largest exporter of the commodity.

In the 1960s many smallholders diversified away from an exclusive concentration on the national staple. They began growing other export crops, including maize, tapioca, sugarcane, pineapples and tobacco. Today, Thailand's principal exports after rice, rubber and tin are such agricultural products as these.

Though he was authoritarian and outlawed opposition to his regime, Sarit won popularity through his economic achievements. He was also astute enough to harness both religion and

136

the monarchy to enhance his own legitimacy. A series of laws organized the *sangha*, the order of Buddhist monks, into a multi-layered hierarchy in which each level had direct links with a corresponding level of civil government. Although the structure gave the government tighter control over religious affairs, the monks were acquiescent. Some monks became involved in government programmes, and went on missions among the hill peoples to convert them to Buddhism and elicit their loyalty to the State.

Meanwhile, the King assumed a more public role than had been customary since 1932; all the ritual of old reappeared. Though the Thais no longer thought of their rulers as divine, they continued to bear them a profound respect and affection.

After Sarit's death in 1963, American presence and influence continued to grow. Many military bases were built around the country, and much of the air war against Vietnam and Laos was conducted from them. In addition, hundreds of thousands of American servicemen passed through Thailand on "rest and recreation" visits.

American military expenditure helped the Thai economy to boom. Meanwhile, Japan began to invest heavily in Thailand and soon became the country's largest trading partner. Banks and luxury hotels proliferated; new industries were established; eight-lane bypasses were built around Bangkok while "strategic highways" linked the regions with the rapidly expanding capital.

But not everybody gained from the economic growth of the period. Peasants were among the worst off. The expansion of agricultural production had been achieved largely by bringing

Vendors display plump vegetables and fruits at a floating market in Damnern Saduak, a town south-west of Bangkok. Canals used to be central Thailand's main arteries; even today, the country's 1,600 kilometres of waterways remain vital for transport and trade.

137

6

virgin land under the plough. Techniques were still labour intensive, and farmers had not benefited from even a modest version of the Green Revolution that had brought prosperity to other ASEAN nations. Though much of the central plain was irrigated, there were few large-scale schemes elsewhere in the country.

In the late 1960s, poor farmers, particularly in the north, the north-east and the south, grew increasingly resentful towards the government's lack of commitment to rural development. In their frustration, the disadvantaged farmers were attracted for a time by the Communist Party of Thailand. Founded in 1942, the Party had for most of the intervening years been banned and obliged to operate clandestinely. In 1965 it began to put into effect a policy of armed insurrection.

Ignoring the predicament of the farmers, the Thai government reacted vigorously against the symptoms of their alienation. Within only a few years, most of Thailand's 75 provinces were declared zones of Communist infiltration. Counter-insurgency now became the watchword, and even the monks were encouraged to give anti-Communist sermons.

Meanwhile, the universities became another focus of discontent. Many of the students had become critical of foreign economic and cultural influences and began to be aware of the conditions of urban and rural workers, with whom they were making contact for the first time.

A movement for the reinstatement and reform of the Constitution, which had been abrogated after a coup in 1971, attracted widespread support. In October 1973 there were massive demonstrations on the streets of Bangkok.

Government troops opened fire on the crowds—an action without precedent in the country's history—and scores of protestors were killed. The King at once took a hand to prevent further bloodshed. Deprived of his support, the two leading military men in the government had to leave the country.

With their departure a long period of authoritarian rule came to an end and a series of civilian governments followed. New political parties campaigned openly, progressive journals multiplied, left-wing students made their voices heard. Parliament, res-

ponding to popular wishes, legislated on agricultural rents for the minority of peasants who were not freeholders.

A radical realignment of foreign policy took place, reflecting not only the climate within Thailand but also a new external reality. The Vietnam War had ended and Communist governments now ruled Laos, Cambodia and Vietnam. The Thais recognized that they would do well to be on reasonable terms with their Communist neighbours, however distasteful their regimes. Seeking connections with the nearest superpower that might support it against Vietnamese aggression,

Thailand opened diplomatic relations with China in 1975. Responding to left-wing demands and also pragmatically recognizing that relations with Vietnam would be easier if links with the United States were loosened, the Thai government asked the Americans to close down their military bases in the country. The Americans, disillusioned by the Vietnam War and in any case well ensconced in the Philippines, agreed. By 1976, the last American air and naval units had departed.

Although Thailand was enacting radical changes, the new mood of the country was far from unanimously held. Many senior military and civilian conservatives were anxious to undermine the civilian government so that the army could take over once more. A vicious reaction to the regime set in. A number of paramilitary groups of village thugs, some with the army or the police behind them, harassed the meetings of students and farmers. Dozens of politicians and trade unionists were assassinated.

The tactics succeeded. Early in 1976, the tensions within the ruling coalition forced the Prime Minister, Kukrit Pramoj, to resign. The succeeding government was demoralized and unable to stem the rising tide of violence. Taking advantage of the chaos, 24 army officers staged a military *coup d'état* against the elected government on October 6, 1976.

The year that followed the October 1976 coup was one of extraordinary political extremism by Thai standards. Farmers' and workers' groups were suppressed; there were political trials; books and newspapers were banned and burnt. Many intellectuals sought refuge abroad; a few thousand students and others "went to the jungle" to join

A colourful headdress distinguishes a young Akha girl from her counterparts among the hill peoples of northern Thailand. As she grows older, the girl will add more decorations; when she reaches adulthood, she will adorn it with all the silver she can afford.

the Communist-led guerrillas, and the anti-government insurrection renewed its intensity.

A more normal political climate was re-established when a new generation of reformist army officers, known as the "Young Turks", promoted to the premiership first General Kriangsak and then, in 1980, another recently retired officer, former Commander-in-Chief General Prem Tinsulanond. Soon after taking power, the latter offered the guerrillas an amnesty to return from the jungle to the cities.

Thousands took up the offer and the Communist Party, simultaneously undermined by internal divisions and lack of external support, declined drastically in size and influence.

Prem introduced a largely civilian administration, which was far more liberal than any of its predecessors save those between 1973 and 1976. The army accepted the shift, albeit reluctantly. Military *coups d'état*, in some postwar periods in Thailand almost biennial events, became rather less frequent and decidedly less successful.

Some senior generals still proclaimed a mission to act as caretakers in the endlessly extended transition to democracy, but others began to advocate a more straightforwardly professional role for the military.

Even under Prem's rule, Thailand remained a good way from democracy: senior ministers were not required to be elected and the Senate, the upper house of parliament, was appointed. But the lower house was elected and many observers were hopeful that by the mid-1980s the country was capable

On a misty morning, an Akha woman returns to her bamboo-and-thatch village with a basket of banana stems to feed her pigs. Like most of the other minorities inhabiting the hills of northern Thailand, the Akha have traditionally practised an independent, semi-nomadic way of life.

6

of moving towards a more genuinely parliamentary form of government.

More than 80 per cent of Thailand's population live in the countryside and pay little attention to political dramas in Bangkok. For centuries, village life has been the main reality. Though the proportion of the agricultural labour force has declined from 88 per cent in the early 1950s to less than 70 per cent in the late 1980s, the absolute number of farmers has increased in step with Thailand's rapid population growth.

So far, Thailand has easily accommodated the burgeoning rural population, since until recently vast tracts had never been cultivated. A century ago half the land was forested, though today the figure is down to below 20 per cent. The Thais have always been a relatively mobile people; when an area becomes crowded, a few inhabitants set off on their own and found a new community on the forest fringe. One consequence of this pattern of settlement is that most Thai villages are less than a hundred years old.

The pioneers look for a spot where wet-rice cultivation is possible, usually near a river. When they find it, they set about establishing themselves not just physically but also spiritually in their forest abode. To them, the hills and the trees, the waters and the subsoil are the habitat of numerous spirits which have to be exorcised, placated or enlisted to help them in their practical endeavours. The Thais do not see this nature worship as distinct from their Buddhism. Some of their beliefs about the invisible beings around them probably originated in Thailand's pre-Buddhist days, but they have been effortlessly blended with Buddha's teachings.

Housebuilding, one of the villagers' first tasks, reveals sharply their concern to achieve harmony with nature and where possible to subdue it. Auspicious times and locations for building are selected by experts, usually men who have been inmates of a monastery for a while, who refer to textbooks on such matters. The timber

Workers turn out pencils in a factory outside Bangkok—a smaller-scale offshoot of Thailand's large forest industry. Foreign demand for teak and other species, coupled with domestic land clearance and consumption of timber for firewood, saw the forested area halved between 1961 and 1985.

chosen for the main house posts is rid of its spirit inhabitant by means of offerings and incantations, and given a soul and an honorific title. The floor of the house is built well off the ground to lift the dwellers away from insects, floods and hostile spirits.

Traditional houses have bamboo or teak walls surrounded by wide verandas and a roof of plaited leaves, grass or wooden shingles. Although there are always some walled rooms entered by a door, the entrance to the house itself is not sealed by a door or other barrier and there are only gaps for windows.

The village pioneers cut down and burn a patch of forest and grow rice and vegetables on the plot they have created. On their death, their land is divided equally between their sons and daughters; the next generation may in its turn clear more land, probably farther from the village. In the meantime, married daughters live in their parents' home with their husbands and share the work in the fields and house. Within the household, the women have considerable authority—more than in Malay societies—and they participate equally in most tasks.

In the past, villagers recall nostalgically, every household would help the others in building houses, planting and harvesting the rice crop. Nowadays, the habit of co-operation is dwindling, but villagers still participate in each other's celebrations and rites of passage, not least by bringing food and helping to cook for numerous household feasts. Neighbours visit each other frequently to exchange news, banter and expressions of affection.

Even the most casual visit is governed by decorous rules of politeness and etiquette. It is the host who must thank departing guests—rather than

An elephant lines up teak logs in a northern forest. Some 5,000 domesticated elephants work in Thailand's forest industry, hauling trees across ground often too rough for machines. Several thousand wild elephants roam the national parks.

6

vice versa—for the honour of the visit. Great respect is accorded to elders; even a small age difference matters. The younger of two friends addresses the other as "older sibling" and is careful always to initiate the greeting.

Not long after a village is founded, the elders will propose building a temple. Nobody is likely to demur, since constructing a place of worship and providing for monks are among the acts of piety thought to bring the greatest spiritual merit to the giver, and no little social esteem. Villagers are prepared to work immensely hard and make many material sacrifices for the sake of their shrine.

Initially they may merely construct a hut with a fence around it for a monk to sleep in. Later they will build a meeting hall and install an image of the Buddha. If the community grows, it will continue to elaborate the edifice, adding a sacred chapel and perhaps a cloister. There are celebrations to dedicate each stage and to attract contributions from villages far and wide. The householders provide the monks' daily food and the necessities for the year-round succession of holy days.

Those who enter the temple as monks are villagers themselves, albeit elevated to a sacred status by the ritual of ordination. Some may remain members of the Buddhist order of monks for several years, or indeed all their lives. Most, however, serve only for a three-month period once in their lives, perhaps just before marriage. Often they choose the rainy season—the growing period for the main rice crop—when there is little work in the fields. The decision is up to the individual, who may leave at any time.

The temple is central to the lives of all the villagers. They attend it to listen to the scriptures, to make vows and offerings, and also to discuss secular matters.

It is in the sacred compound that processional floats for festivals are made, there that drums and gongs are stored and practised. Some monks may be expert in giving medical, astrological or other counsel. All are available to perform domestic rituals, chanting scriptures in the house of the dead and leading the funeral bier to the cremation ground.

Nowadays, villages are not isolated from the outside world as they were as recently as the 1960s. Buses and trucks allow most villagers to make a day trip to the nearest market town, where once the journey might have taken a week. There government influence will be present in the shape of the District Office, which houses land records, the registry of births, marriages and deaths, and the army recruiting office.

Other urban influences have begun to change the look of Thai villages. Many houses now have doors with locks and

shuttered windows; the wealthy build two-storey homes of brick. Young people generally wear Western dress. Electricity has reached some communities, and the well-to-do own fans, refrigerators and television sets. Village committees and offices proliferate according to bewildering ministerial plans. Where once there might only have been groups concerned with the temple and perhaps irrigation, there are now also bodies supervising schools and land development, farming co-operatives, defence volunteers and organizations for young people.

While the intrusion of the State and the market into rural life has in a sense drawn country people into a closer relationship with national society, it has also created new gulfs within the villages themselves. Two decades of planned development have created a new local élite of office-holders, traders, building contractors, moneylenders, landlords and owners of trucks and agricultural machinery. Starting only marginally better-placed than their neighbours in terms of land-holding or office, they have capitalized on the greatly increased opportunities for trading and hobnobbing with officials. Members of this group predominate in the committees, and often take the law into their own hands when dealing with less well-placed neighbours. Thai traditions of deference to those higher up in the hierarchy bolster their power.

Many escape rural poverty and dependence by seeking work elsewhere. Some villages, especially in the north-east, seem to contain only the children and the old who have been left behind. Those Thais who can scrape together the cost of travelling and labour-brokers' fees head for the Middle East, Malaysia or Singapore. In some years the value of the annual remittances of Thais working abroad equals that of the entire rice export. The alternative is to make for the towns. Most urban workers are first or second-generation peasants. Bangkok, where industry and commerce are concentrated, is the goal for the majority.

The capital has a population of over five million and is 20 times larger than the next biggest city—Chiang Mai in the north. Built on both sides of the Chao Phraya river, Bangkok is criss-crossed with canals which flood the streets and ground floors of houses annually. In the past there were many more canals, but the majority have been filled in and transformed into roads. Even so, traffic problems still plague the city. In the streets, rickshaw drivers compete for survival with innumerable small trucks bringing market produce from the surrounding country, with buses packed to overflowing, and the air-conditioned, black-windowed, chauffeur-driven limousines of the privileged élite. Only the imminent passage of a royal procession—in white or yellow Daimlers and Mercedes—produces a respectful hush. The streets are cleared and building workers urged to descend from their scaffolding, more to avoid the impropriety of being higher than the king than for security reasons.

The many fine temples and palaces, old ministerial buildings in classical European style and rows of shops with living space above, which were the chief architectural features of the city until the 1960s, have been overshadowed by massive new office blocks, hotels and shopping centres. But the main thoroughfares are still humanized by tens of thousands of street vendors.

Some hawk their goods from place to place. Snack-sellers manoeuvre bicycles adapted to carry large display cabinets and huge umbrellas. Indians carry trays of assorted nuts on their heads; Chinese peddle steamed muffins and fried soya bean curd. Others set up stalls outside shops, along canals or under raised sections of motorway, strongly resisting periodic official attempts to drive them off the streets in the interests of tidying up the capital. Among them are sun-darkened villagers, in brightly coloured sarongs and broad-brimmed farmer's hats, who have travelled in for the day by bus or truck. They carry what they can—including, if need be, a charcoal stove—in two baskets slung at either end of a whippy bamboo shoulder pole. There is an occasional astrologer or a young north-easterner selling traditional cushions, but most stallholders cater for the Thais' prodigious fondness for snacks. They sell rice delicacies wrapped in banana leaves or cooked in bamboo tubes, hot cakes freshly baked on charcoal, flattened dried squid, hot spicy noodles. And they capitalize on the wonderful variety of fresh fruit found throughout the region, offering juice to drink, preserved fruits, mangoes with rice and coconut cream, or pineapple served with the crushed ice that seems to be available everywhere.

Some of the first-generation city-dwellers survive even more precariously than the street vendors. More than a million children aged between seven and 11 are engaged in production, often in small urban sweatshops. Thousands keep alive scavenging on rubbish tips or recycling discarded bags and bottles. Figures for female prostitution in Thailand range from half a million to double that, of whom a large fraction are in Bangkok.

Thai society has always condoned prostitution but it was in the Vietnam War years, when thousands of servicemen passed through on rest and recreation trips, that sex became big business. Now it has become a key ingredient in Thailand's appeal to tourists. Relishing the foreign exchange it draws in, the authori-

Rush-hour traffic chokes a street in Bangkok, which accommodates 90 per cent of the country's motor vehicles. To ease congestion, the government has initiated a number of projects including a ring road, an elevated expressway and an overhead railway.

143

6

A Thai Muslim—a member of the
country's largest religious minority—
walks past a fleet of ornately decorated
fishing boats beached outside a village
on the south-east coast. Fish, mainly
mackerel, accounts for more than half
the protein in the national diet.

ties have turned a blind eye to the lurid nightlife of Bangkok and the other cities, and give scant thought to the social costs. Most of the prostitutes are under 18, and one in 10 is less than 13. Most come from distant villages and are at the mercy of the pimps who recruit them as they alight from the trains into the cities. Some become virtual slaves, receiving nothing beyond their meagre daily meals.

Not all of the newcomers to the cities fall into such desperate straits. Many find real opportunities for advancement. The economic growth of the past three decades has created thousands of new jobs in retailing, service industries, computers and many other fields. Those who have taken advantage of the openings and groomed their children for yet higher things are rapidly swelling the ranks of the middle class, which traditionally was a very limited group, composed of Chinese businessmen and Thai officials. Increasingly educated and well travelled, the members of today's middle class admire Western habits and institutions. Their clothes and possessions are Western, though they retain their Buddhism and their ingrained habits of politeness and deference.

Members of the burgeoning middle class are frustrated by Thailand's highly personalized politics, which leaves their own views little scope for expression. They aspire to succeed the generals in power and to introduce a civilian democratic polity. Until a *modus vivendi* is established between these educated, articulate dissenters and the army, Thai politics will lack stability. But whatever the outcome of today's uncertainties, it will surely be marked by the grace and endurance of the Thai people

The same qualities may aid Thailand in its quest for peace with its neighbours. Thailand can never afford to forget that it is a front-line state, facing the potentially belligerent Vietnamese across its eastern border. But the country that collaborated with the Japanese during World War II and yet ended the war on good terms with the Allies has not lost its nimbleness. Today it attempts cordial relations with powers of every political complexion. The Americans, though they left their bases in 1976, have, ever since the Vietnamese invasion of Cambodia in 1979, supplied massive military aid. And since 1975, relations with China have been warm.

But perhaps the most valued of Thailand's friends are its partners in ASEAN. Culturally the Thais, with their monarchy, their religion and their history of feuds with the Vietnamese, are some distance from the other ASEAN nations. On the other hand, Thailand has had no quarrel with any other ASEAN country, whereas several of the others have been at loggerheads until recently.

The country has yet to benefit substantially from the tentative attempts at economic co-operation within ASEAN and there is no guarantee that any of the other countries would come to Thailand's aid militarily if it was invaded. Yet it is these countries who most closely share Thai interests; Thailand feels stronger and more secure for its links with neighbouring non-Communist countries in an explosive part of the world. It has long been accepted in ASEAN that special weight should be attached to the views of Thailand, its only front-line state, in formulating its diplomatic policy. ASEAN members collectively have made far more world impact than Thailand could alone when condemning destabilizing forces in the region, notably Vietnam's invasion of Cambodia in 1979. Ever pragmatic and increasingly co-operative, the countries of ASEAN face their common destiny with courage and optimism.

A line of shaven-headed novices waits
at the temple steps to receive food
from passing laymen. Normally the
monks must go out into the town with
their bowls to seek alms, but this is a
festival day in the Buddhist calendar,
when townspeople will throng
Haripunchai's compound to worship.

MONASTIC LIFE IN THAILAND

The ancient Buddhist temple of Haripunchai is the greatest treasure of the town of Lamphun in northern Thailand. Like its counterparts across the nation, it draws the monks that live in it from the local populace; it is normally home to a brotherhood of about 40 adults and 70 novices, teenagers attending the temple school. After sojourning there for a few months or years, most will return to the world.

The monks see their spell in the temple as an opportunity to strive for perfection. Buddhism teaches that reincarnation follows death, and that only by living according to the highest standards can a person ever escape the wearisome round of death and rebirth. Recognizing how hard it is for a lay person to obey such maxims as never harming another creature, most Thai men enter a monastery at least once in their lives. Their lay brethren express their own religious feelings by supporting the monks with gifts.

A plan of Haripunchai executed by a teacher in the temple school reveals a typical disposition of temple buildings. The monk's quarters and the schoolrooms are near the perimeter. In the central area stand holy structures, including the *chedi*—a spire which enshrines a relic of the Buddha.

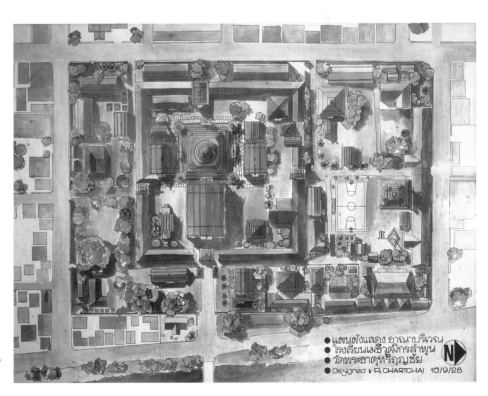

Young monks pass in front of the
sacred *chedi*, the oldest building in the
temple. Its base dates back to the 10th
or 11th century; the bell-shaped dome
of burnished copper was rebuilt
several times in later centuries.

In the incense-laden chiaroscuro of the prayer hall, a visiting layman kneels before multiple images of the Buddha. His solitary act of devotion is characteristic of Buddhism's emphasis on inwardness: although the monks pray together each evening, communal worship for lay people is rare.

Novices and lay children share a classroom of the temple school. Unlike state-run secondary education, the school at Haripunchai is free. Three quarters of the pupils live here or in other nearby monasteries, the rest come in each day from the town.

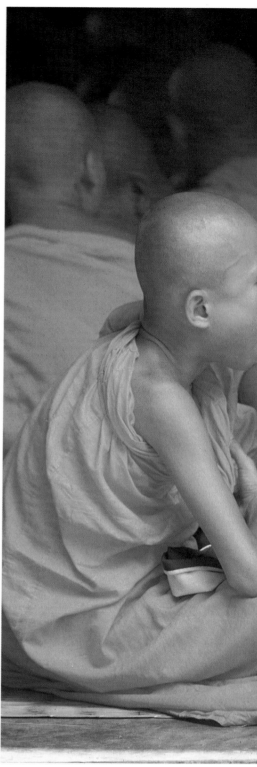

Soon after dawn, a woman bows to show her respect for a pair of alms-seeking monks who have just accepted her gift of rice. Regular givers know the monks' routes and wait in the same spot daily with their contributions.

Young novices pool and consume the food they have been given. Inmates may eat only between sunrise and noon; they normally have one meal on their return from their dawn alms-collection round and another at the end of the morning.

At a ceremony in a private house in Lamphun, chanting monks bless the building, its owner, her dead parents and all her ancestors. The far end of the cord they hold charges a bowl of holy water with their collected prayers. Some will be sprinkled over the guests, and the rest kept by the householder.

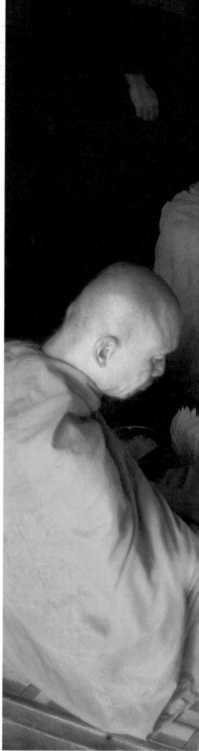

Once the ceremony is over, the monks
sit down to a lavish meal, prepared by
the householder as recompense for
their services. Through their holy
ministrations, she will have gained
spiritual merit, and is expected to pay
accordingly for the benefits.

Within the temple compound, a young monk and his companions bask in the afternoon sun. Monks are not confined to their quarters: as long as they are present for meals, prayers and lessons, they are free at other times and may wander in the town as they please.

ACKNOWLEDGEMENTS

The index for this book was prepared by Vicki Robinson. For their help in the preparation of this volume, the editors wish to thank the following: The Abbot of Wat Phrathat Haripunchai, Lamphun, Thailand; Sonny Aguirre, Manila; Guy Andrews, London; Judy Aspinall, London; British Council for Aid to Refugees, London; Mike Brown, London; Siriporn Buranaphan, Bangkok; Inson Charoenporn, Chiang Mai, Thailand; Windsor Chorlton, London; Alan Croghan, USIS, U.S. Embassy, Manila; A. Dewey, Total Oil, London; Dr. Constante N. Firme, Dr. José Fabella Memorial Hospital, Manila; Felicia Freeland, London; Friends of the Earth, London; Cherrie Gross, London; Helen Grubin, London; Andy Hernandes, Manila; Joanna Hucker, London; Shuib Hussain, Tourist Development Corporation, Penang, Malaysia; Indonesian Embassy, London; International Press Centre, Manila; Isra Jerachaisakdecha, Chiang Mai, Thailand; Lt. Daniel P. Lachica, 20th Air Commando Squadron, Villamor Air Base, Pasay City, Philippines; Kate Cann, Guildford, Surrey, England; Cindy Lilles, Manila Hotel, Manila; R. A. Longmire, Bookham, Surrey, England; Malaysian High Commission, London; Davide and Carla Manfreddi, Bali; R. W. Sasminta Mardawa, Yogyakarta, Indonesia; Anton Neumann, London; Susan Ooi, London; Capt. Norbie Panganiban, 20th Air Commando Squadron, Villamore Air Base, Pasay City, Philippines; Roy Perrott, London; Elizabeth Plint, Oxford, England; Prince G. P. Poeroeboyo, Yogyakarta, Indonesia; Sally Rowland, Saffron Walden, Essex, England; Andrew Sarao, Manila; Asad Shiraz, Singapore Tourist Promotion Board, Singapore; Singapore High Commission, London; Singapore Tourist Promotion Board, London; Grace de Solo, Manila; Sri Sultan Hamengkubuwono 1X of Yogyakarta; Tjokorda Gde Putra Sukawati, Bali; Pichai Suranantsri, Bangkok; Agus Suwito, Yogyakarta, Indonesia; David Tan, London; Thai Embassy, London; Tourism Authority of Thailand, Bangkok; Sandro Tucci, Manila; Bodge Wallingford, Chiang Mai, Thailand; Apichart Weerawong, Bangkok.

PICTURE CREDITS

Credits from left to right are separated by semicolons, from top to bottom by dashes.

Cover: Juergen Schmitt from The Image Bank, London. Front endpaper: Map by Roger Stewart, London. Back endpaper: Digitized image by Ralph Scott/Chapman Bounford, London.

1, 2: © Flag Research Center, Winchester, Massachusetts, U.S.A. 6, 7: Graham Grieves from Robert Harding Picture Library, London. (Digitized images by Ralph Scott/Chapman Bounford, London.) 8, 9: Amos Schliack from Focus, Hamburg. (Digitized image by Ralph Scott/Chapman Bounford, London.) 10, 11: Michael Freeman, London. (Digitized image by Ralph Scott/Chapman Bounford, London.) 12, 13: Hans Hoefer from APA Photo Agency, Singapore. 14–17: Michael Freeman, London. 18: Michael Freeman, London; Barbara Gundle, Portland, Oregon, U.S.A.; Marlane Guelden, Kuala Lumpur. 19: Michael Freeman, London; Vautier-de-Nanxe, Paris; Michael Freeman, London. 20: Vautier-de-Nanxe, Paris. 21: Michael MacIntyre from The Hutchison Library, London. 22: Rainer Drexel from Bilderberg, Hamburg. 25: Hans Hoefer from APA Photo Agency, Singapore. 26: Lyle Lawson, London. 28: 'Opperkoopman voc & retourboot op de rede van Batavia' by Aelbert Cuyp, courtesy of the Rijksmuseum, Amsterdam. 29: Michael Freeman, London. 30: Anne Conway, Paris. 31: Courtesy of the Imperial War Museum, London. 32, 33: J. Henebry, Wilmette, Illinois, U.S.A. 34: Amos Schliack from Focus, Hamburg. 36: Michael Freeman, London. 37: Dr. Georg Gerster from The John Hillelson Picture Agency, London. 38, 39: Joseph Viesti from Agence ANA, Paris. 40: Kal Müller from APA Photo Agency, Singapore. 41: Michael Freeman, London. 42: Courtesy of the Victoria and Albert Museum, London (IM 147-1921); 'Iacatara (Djakarta)' from '*Livro do Estado da India Oriental*', 1646, courtesy of The British Library, London; Paul Conklin from Camera Press, London. 44: Sybil Sassoon from Robert Harding Picture Library, London. 46: Michael Freeman, London. 47: G. P. Reichelt, Hamburg. 49: Vautier-de-Nanxe, Paris—Sybil Sassoon from Robert Harding Picture Library, London. 50, 51: D. and J. Heaton from Colorific!, London. 53: Sybil Sassoon from Robert Harding Picture Library, London. 54: Vautier-de-Nanxe, Paris. 55: Gregory Lawler, Portland, Oregon, U.S.A. 56, 57: John Egan, The Hutchison Library, London. 58–67, Michael Freeman, London. 68: David Liddle from Horizon International Photographic Agency, Sydney. 69: Lyle Lawson, London. 70, 71: Anthony Howarth from Susan Griggs Agency, London. 72: Lyle Lawson, London—Gunther Deichmann, Darwin, Australia (2). 73: Michael Freeman, London. 74, 75: Amos Schliack from Focus, Hamburg. 77: 'Alfonso de Albuquerque' from *Livro do Estado da India Oriental*, 1646, courtesy of The British Library, London; oil on canvas by F. Grant (detail), 1847, courtesy of the National Portrait Gallery, London; Map Research Center, Winchester, Massachusetts, U.S.A.—Courtesy of the National Maritime Museum, London. 78: Margaret Collier from Robert Harding Picture Library, London. 79: Michael Freeman, London. 80: David Alan Harvey from Woodfin Camp Inc., Washington, D.C. 81: Lance Nelson from Horizon International Photographic Agency, Sydney. 82: Michael Freeman, London. 83: David Alan Harvey from Susan Griggs Agency, London. 85: Raghubir Singh from Agence ANA, Paris. 86, 87: Lyle Lawson, London. 88: Adam Woolfitt from Susan Griggs Agency, London. 89: R. Ian Lloyd from APA Photo Agency, Singapore. 90, 91: Patrick Ward, London. 92: Oil on canvas by G. F. Joseph (detail), 1817, courtesy of The National Portrait Gallery, London. 93: Lithograph by J. T. Thompson, photo by Philip Little from APA Photo Agency, Singapore. 94: R. Ian Lloyd from APA Photo Agency, Singapore. 96: Michael Freeman, London. 97–99: Adam Woolfitt from Susan Griggs Agency, London. 100, 101: Michael Freeman, London. 102: Piers Cavendish from Reflex Picture Agency, London. 103: Christopher Bain, Port Washington, New York. 104: Alain Evrard from Susan Griggs Agency, London. 105: Professor Charles Boxer, Little Gaddensden, Hertfordshire, England; courtesy of *Punch*, London—Piers Cavendish from Reflex Picture Agency, London. 106–109: Michael Freeman, London. 110–111: Ted Spiegel from Susan Griggs Agency, London. 112: Piers Cavendish from Reflex Picture Agency, London. 115: Harald Sund, Seattle, Washington, U.S.A. 116, 117: Robert Frerck from Odyssey Productions, Chicago, Illinois, U.S.A. 118–130: Michael Freeman, London. 131: Gunther Deichmann, Darwin, Australia. 132: Michael Freeman, London. 134: Ann and Bury Peerless, Birchington-on-Sea, Kent, England. 135: Werner Forman Archive, London; 'King Mongkut' from *Louis and the King of Siam* by Dr. W. S. Bristowe, courtesy of Mrs. Belinda Brocklehurst, Tunbridge Wells, Kent, England. 136–139: Michael Freeman, London. 140: Jean Guy Jules from Agence ANA, Paris. 141: Jim Howard from Colorific!, London. 142: Amos Schliack from Focus, Hamburg. 144, 145: Lyle Lawson, London. 146–155: Michael Freeman, London.

BIBLIOGRAPHY

BOOKS

Allen, Charles, *Tales from the South China Seas.* British Broadcasting Corporation, André Deutsch, London, 1983.

Andaya, Barbara J. Watson, and Andaya, Leonard Y., *A History of Malaysia.* St. Martin's, N.Y., 1984.

Anima, Nid, *In Defense of Cockfighting.* Omar Publications, Quezon City, Philippines, 1977.

Bedlington, Stanley S., *Malaysia and Singapore.* Cornell University Press, Ithaca, N.Y., 1978.

Bunge, Frederica M., ed., *Malaysia: a country study.* Foreign Area Studies, The American University, Washington, D.C., 1984.

Bunge, Frederica M., ed., *Philippines: a country study.* Foreign Area Studies, The American University, Washington, D.C., 1984.

Bunge, Frederica M., ed., *Thailand: a country study.* Foreign Area Studies, The American University, Washington, D.C., 1981.

Bunnag, Jane, *Buddhist Monk, Buddhist Layman: A Study of Urban Monastic Organisation in Central Thailand.* Cambridge University Press, 1973.

Choy, Lee Khoon, *Indonesia: Between Myth and Reality.* Nile & Mackenzie Ltd., London, 1976.

Constantino, Renato, *A History of the Philippines.* Monthly Review Press, New York and London, 1975.

Dalton, Bill, *Indonesia Handbook.* Moon Publications, Chico, Calif., 1980.

Dutt, Ashok K., ed., *Southeast Asia — Realm of Contrasts.* Westview Press Inc., Boulder, Colo., 1985.

Eurasia Media Co. Ltd., *Kaleidoscope: Indonesia Meeting The 21st Century.* Hong Kong, 1984.

Far Eastern Economic Review Ltd., *Asia 1985 Yearbook.* Hong Kong, 1985.

Farmer, B. H., *An Introduction to South Asia.* Methuen Inc., New York, 1984.

Fisher, Charles A., *South-East Asia, A Social, Economic and Political Geography.* Methuen Inc., New York, 1966.

Flower, Raymond, *Raffles: The Story of Singapore.* Croom Helm, Kent, 1984.

Geertz, Clifford, *Agricultural Involution: Indonesia.* University of California Press, Berkeley, Calif., 1963.

Gorospe, Vitaliano R., and Deats, Richard L., *The Filipino in the Seventies.* New Day Publishers, Quezon City, Philippines, 1973.

Grant, Bruce, *Indonesia.* Cambridge University Press, London, 1964.

Haditjaroko, Sunardjo, *Ramayana, Indonesia Wayang Show.* Penerbit Djambatari, Jakarta, 1981.

Hanks, Lucien M., *Rice & Man: Ecology in Southeast Asia.* Aldine Atterton Inc., Chicago, 1972.

Hunter, Guy, *South-East Asia — Race, Culture and Nation.* Oxford University Press, New York, 1966.

Indonesia. Insight Guide, Prentice-Hall, Englewood Cliffs, N.J., 1984.

Jocano, F. Landa, *Slum as a Way of Life.* University of the Philippines Press, Quezon City, Philippines, 1975.

Josey, Alex, *Singapore: its Past, Present and Future.* André Deutsch Ltd., London, 1980.

Khoo, Gilbert, *A History of South-East Asia since 1500.* Oxford University Press, Kuala Lumpur, 1970.

Legge, J. D., *Sukarno, A Political Biography.* Allen & Unwin Inc., Winchester, Mass., 1985.

Lewis, Elaine, and Lewis, Paul, *Peoples of the Golden Triangle, Six Tribes in Thailand.* Thames and Hudson, New York, 1984.

Malaysia. Insight Guide, Prentice Hall, Englewood Cliffs, N.J., 1984.

Miller, Russell, and the Editors of Time-Life Books, *The East Indiamen* (The Seafarers series). Time-Life International, Amsterdam, 1980.

Moebirman, *Wayang Purwa, the Shadow Play of Indonesia.* Yayasan Pelita Wisata, Jakarta, 1973.

Nelson, Raymond, *The Philippines.* Thames and Hudson Ltd., London, 1968.

Osborne, Milton, *Southeast Asia: An Introductory History.* Allen & Unwin Inc., Winchester, Mass., 1985.

Palmier, Leslie, *Indonesia.* Thames and Hudson Ltd., London, 1965.

Philippines. Insight Guide, Prentice-Hall, Englewood Cliffs, N.J., 1983.

Ricklefs, Merle C., *A History of Modern Indonesia.* The Macmillan Press Ltd., London, 1981.

Ryan, Neil J., *A History of Malaysia and Singapore.* Oxford University Press, Kuala Lumpur, 1976.

Scoble, Henry M., and Wiseberg, Laurie S., eds., *Access to Justice: Human Rights Struggles in South East Asia.* Zed Books Ltd., London, 1985.

Sien, Chia Lin, and MacAndrews, Colin, eds., *Southeast Asian Seas, Frontiers for Development.* McGraw-Hill International Book Company, Singapore, 1981.

Sievers, Allen M., *The Mystical World of Indonesia: Culture and Economic Development in Conflict.* The Johns Hopkins University Press, Baltimore, 1974.

Singapore. Insight Guide, Prentice-Hall, Englewood Cliffs, N.J., 1983.

Steinberg, David Joel, ed., *In Search of Southeast Asia.* Univ. of Hawaii Press, Honolulu, 1985.

Steinberg, Rafael, and the Editors of Time-Life Books, *Return to the Philippines* (World War II series). Time-Life Books, Alexandria, Va., 1979.

Sutlive, J. R., and Vinson, H., *The Iban of Sarawak.* AHM Publishing Corporation, Ill., 1978.

Taylor, John Gelman, *The Social World of Batavia, European and Eurasian in Dutch Asia.* The University of Wisconsin Press, Madison, 1983.

Thailand. Insight Guide, Prentice-Hall, Englewood Cliffs, N.J., 1984.

Thailand Angkor (Cambodia). Nagel, Geneva, 1973.

Thailand into the 80s. Published by the Office of the Prime Minister, Bangkok, 1980.

The Japanese Occupation: Singapore 1942-1945. Archives and Oral History Department, News and Publication Ltd., Singapore, 1985.

Torres, Emmanuel, *Jeepney.* GCF Books, Quezon City, Philippines, 1979.

Vreeland, Nena, *Area Handbook for Singapore.* Foreign Area Studies, The American University, Washington, D.C., 1977.

Wheeler, Tony, *South-East Asia on a Shoestring.* Lonely Planet Publications, Emeryville, Calif., 1985.

World Development Report 1984. The World Bank, Oxford University Press, New York, 1984.

Zich, Arthur, and the Editors of Time-Life Books, *The Rising Sun* (World War II series). Time-Life Books, Alexandria, Va., 1977.

PERIODICALS

"Alike but different", *Far Eastern Economic Review,* April 18, 1985.

"Ancient Magic", *Connoisseur,* November, 1985.

"Asean", *The Times,* April 30, 1984.

"A Test for Democracy", *Time,* February 3, 1986.

"File on the Philippines", *Departures,* January–February, 1985.

"Indonesia, *Financial Times,* April 30, 1984.

"Indonesia: Suharto steps out", *The World Today,* October, 1985.

"Monsoons", *National Geographic,* December, 1984.

"Poverty in Indonesia", *World Bank Staff Working Papers,* no. 671, 1984.

"Singapore", *Financial Times,* December 12, 1984.

"Singapore's Success Story", *New Leader,* August 12, 1985.

"The Chinese in Indonesia, The Philippines and Malaysia", *Minority Rights Group,* Report No. 10, revised 1982 edition.

"The Filipinos", *Asiaweek,* November 29, 1985.

"The Malaysians", *Asiaweek,* May 10, 1985.

"The Philippines Search for Identity", *Asian Affairs,* October 1985.

"The Strange Case of Singapore", *Geo,* November, 1984.

"West Irian, East Timor and Indonesia", *Minority Rights Group,* Report No. 42, 1979.

INDEX

Colour separations by Fotolitomec, S.N.C., Milan, Italy.
Typesetting by Tradespools Ltd., Somerset, England.